P...

Divine Applause

"God's love isn't based on our performance. But He does want us to actively engage with Him, to get His 'attention' through prayer, devotion, and acts of service. *Divine Applause* offers practical guidance to help readers make that a deeper reality in their lives."

—JIM DALY, president of Focus on the Family

"Jeff Anderson reminds us that God doesn't just sit in the bleachers of your life. He's paying close attention. He applauds. He gets involved."

—DOUG BENDER, coauthor of *I Am Second*

"Unlike human applause, 'divine applause' is a receipt, not a bill. Jeff Anderson shows us how to have a real relationship with God that is not based on bill paying but on bountiful receipts of God's favor and pleasure."

—LEONARD SWEET, best-selling author, professor,
and chief contributor to Sermons.com

"Attention is something children will cry for and adults will die for. Jeff Anderson shows us how we can connect with God's blessing and applause."

—JIM STOVALL, best-selling author of *The Ultimate Gift*

"Jeff Anderson has creatively placed our personal experience with God on the lower shelf for all who desire to reach it. This work begs to be read by anyone who wishes to see the invisible God."

—DR. TONY EVANS, president of The Urban Alternative
and senior pastor of Oak Cliff Bible Fellowship

"What a bold encouragement! We are often looking for intimacy with our Creator, and in *Divine Applause* Jeff Anderson illuminates just how close we really are to Him."

—Tom Ziglar, president/CEO of Ziglar, Inc.

"Jeff unpacks the truth about what it means to truly walk alongside the One we call Lord. His creative and intuitive look at the Bible is rejuvenating."

—Jarrid Wilson, next-gen pastor at LifePoint Church

"If you have wondered how you can know Someone you can't see, and if you're curious about what an invisible God thinks of you, then you need to read this book."

—Jeff Goins, author of *The In-Between*

"Jeff Anderson has addressed an issue that many people know intuitively but rarely verbalize: God is invisible. At last we have a book that addresses this reality in a creative, refreshing, and encouraging manner."

—Dr. Richard Blackaby, author of *Unlimiting God*
and coauthor of *Experiencing God*

"Real intimacy with God changes everything, and this book clearly moves people in the right direction. *Divine Applause* appeals to your deep longing for God and takes you on a practical journey."

—Randy Gariss, senior pastor of College Heights
Christian Church

"*Divine Applause* delivers moving stories and fresh insight. This transparent work will satisfy those who want to draw near to God."

—Chuck Bentley, CEO of Crown Financial Ministries

"So many Christians are striving to find a stage, microphone, and lights where they can offer their gifts. Ironically, they miss the connection they long for and the divine applause we were meant to hear."

    —GARY BARKALOW, author of *It's Your Call*

"Jeff's engaging and honest approach will challenge readers to explore more deeply the intimacy of their relationship with God, look for Him in the ordinary moments of life, and make the most of each encounter."

    —MICKEY RAPIER, directional leader at Fellowship Bible
      Church Northwest Arkansas

"To be able to relate to personal stories that introduce biblical insights is absolutely the best. Jeff Anderson has bestowed great joy as I read this book. In your heart you will hear God's divine applause."

    —DR. TED KERSH, author of *The Blessed Life*

"Jeff leads the reader to an honest and true relationship with the Father. He gently lays aside the fallacies we believe about God and ourselves. He reminds believers at every stage that God does delight in you."

    —DR. ALEX HIMAYA, pastor of theCHURCH.at

DIVINE
APPLAUSE

DIVINE APPLAUSE

Secrets and Rewards
of Walking with an Invisible God

JEFF ANDERSON

MULTNOMAH
BOOKS

DIVINE APPLAUSE
PUBLISHED BY MULTNOMAH BOOKS
12265 Oracle Boulevard, Suite 200
Colorado Springs, Colorado 80921

This book is not intended to replace the medical advice of a trained medical professional. Readers are advised to consult a physician or other qualified health-care professional when considering a fast. The author and publisher specifically disclaim liability, loss, or risk, personal or otherwise, which is incurred as a consequence, directly or indirectly, of the use or application of any of the contents of this book.

Scripture quotations are taken from the Holy Bible, New International Version®. NIV®. Copyright © 1973, 1978, 1984 by Biblica Inc.™ Used by permission of Zondervan. All rights reserved worldwide. www.zondervan.com. Scripture quotations marked (ESV) are taken from The Holy Bible, English Standard Version, copyright © 2001 by Crossway Bibles, a division of Good News Publishers. Used by permission. All rights reserved. Scripture quotations marked (KJV) are taken from the King James Version. Scripture quotations marked (NASB) are taken from the New American Standard Bible®. © Copyright The Lockman Foundation 1960, 1962, 1963, 1968, 1971, 1972, 1973, 1975, 1977, 1995. Used by permission. (www.Lockman.org). Scripture quotations marked (NKJV) are taken from the New King James Version®. Copyright © 1982 by Thomas Nelson Inc. Used by permission. All rights reserved.

Italics in Scripture quotations reflect the author's added emphasis.

Details in some anecdotes and stories have been changed to protect the identities of the persons involved.

Trade Paperback ISBN 978-1-60142-530-0
eBook ISBN 978-1-60142-531-7

Cover design by Mark D. Ford; cover photo by Benjamin Rondel/Corbis

Published in the United States by WaterBrook Multnomah, an imprint of the Crown Publishing Group, a division of Random House LLC, New York, a Penguin Random House Company.

MULTNOMAH and its mountain colophon are registered trademarks of Random House LLC.

Library of Congress Cataloging-in-Publication Data
Anderson, Jeff, 1970 February 5–
    Divine applause : secrets and rewards of walking with an invisible God / Jeff Anderson.—First Edition.
       pages cm
       ISBN 978-1-60142-530-0—ISBN 978-1-60142-531-7 (electronic) 1. Spirituality—Christianity.
2. Spiritual life—Christianity. I. Title.
    BV4501.3.A5283 2015
    248.4—dc23

                                                                2014031323

Printed in the United States of America
2015—First Edition

10 9 8 7 6 5 4 3 2 1

SPECIAL SALES
Most WaterBrook Multnomah books are available at special quantity discounts when purchased in bulk by corporations, organizations, and special-interest groups. Custom imprinting or excerpting can also be done to fit special needs. For information, please e-mail SpecialMarkets @WaterBrookMultnomah.com or call 1-800-603-7051.

To my earthly father, Jack Anderson.
Your constant love and attention in my life
have helped me relate to my Heavenly Father.

Contents

Part 3: **WALKING UPWARD**

Acknowledgments

To my wife, Stephanie, for the journey we have shared together and the secrets along the way. The biggest buzzer-shot prayer I ever prayed, God answered. You were the answer.

To my sons, Austin, Cade, and Gunnar, whose stories fill these pages and continue to teach me about being a child and walking with God. You boys make me proud. And you are book stars now, like your sister Autumn.

To my parents, Jack and Lois Anderson, for your love, prayers, and watchful ways when I was young…and still today.

To Matt Benjamin, Monty Cavanagh, Keven Partin, Clay Thompson, and Keith Tracy—your investment and verbal applause for the past decade has sustained me. And to Jeff Hoemann, your encouragement has been refreshing and timely.

To the partners of Acceptable Gift, because of you, I am able to undertake projects like this one.

To the many Roosters in my life, such as Howard Dayton and Chuck Bentley, who have called me out to greater things in my walk with God.

To my agent Mike Loomis, for your Spirit-led vision, wisdom, coaching, counseling, correcting, rebuking (as needed), and editing in helping me to shape this book. You're a true servant, a gift from heaven.

Connecting with a God
We Never See

When does God see us? All the time, right?

But when does God look at us? I mean *really* look.

In my mind, God always sees me. But it seems He's also looking for something...in us. You may have heard this verse before: "For the eyes of the LORD range throughout the earth to strengthen those whose hearts are fully committed to him" (2 Chronicles 16:9).

Besides the imagery of two giant eyeballs galloping around the globe, I'm intrigued by the idea that God looks, and even takes action, in response to us.

Scripture is full of examples. As early as the first generation of earth-born humans, God was caught gazing upon Abel and his gift. There are times God sees a person do (or even think) something and seems to respond with "I'm going to get involved."

Just as we would expect from a loving Father, God is interested in us. When I am with my kids, I always see them. But there are times when they really get my attention. That's when my simple awareness shifts from watching...to focusing on...to gazing at them. At those times I'm often moved to action.

If our Father sees us at all times and in all situations, might there be circumstances that invite His special, focused attention? Could we start living in ways that capture God's attention?

For those who love God, it's a comfort to know we can never drift beyond His sight. King David relished knowing "the eyes of the LORD are on those who fear him, on those whose hope is in his unfailing love" (Psalm 33:18). Jesus reminds us that God enjoys wildflowers and cares about sparrows, but His care for us is far greater.

Unfortunately, these truths can lose impact over time. It's like watching reruns on television. Even if you're watching your favorite program, if you've seen the episode already, it will be less funny, less suspenseful, less captivating.

When we reread familiar passages of Scripture, we can take mindblowing truth for granted: God is always and everywhere seeing us, and He is always and everywhere loving us. We know God can count the grains of sand on every beach, and He knows the number of hairs on your head and mine. We have known these truths since childhood, but sometimes we want more than what the Sunday school answers tell us.

We believe God sees and loves us, and we trust that He notices the details of our lives. But sometimes we want to know—and I mean *really* know—that He delights in us.

After all, what child of God wouldn't long for more direct, more personal encounters with his or her Father?

It's inspiring to read about heroes in Scripture, some of whom were called friends of God (Abraham and Moses), rewarded with a unique description such as "a man after God's own heart" (David), or given new names (Jacob became Israel) after some direct dealings with God.

One thing all of these biblical figures shared in common was an audacious hunger for more. They would not settle for a silent or distant relationship with God. Later on, we will look more closely at the stories of Moses, Gideon, David, John the Baptist, Peter, and many others. (While we're at it, we'll even take a look at Steve, Abraham's servant. Yes, there are some surprises ahead.)

What Do We Desire from Our Father?

We seek God's attention and long to experience a close relationship with Him. Why do we feel, then, that He is not interested or more noticeably involved in our lives? It's because God cannot be seen or heard, at least with our physical senses. But like any dynamic personal connection, walking with God requires two-way engagement. And because we know God to be invisible, we tend to lower our expectations. But no one should be content with a one-sided relationship. God isn't.

I've made it my life's ambition to walk with God, and I continue to be inspired by the story of a man named Enoch. Scriptures don't tell us a lot about him, but one characteristic stands out: he "walked with God" (Genesis 5:24). We know that Enoch never died, in the way we think of death. It seems that he simply walked straight into heaven.

A page later in my Bible I find the story of another man who caught God's attention: Noah, like Enoch, "walked with God" (Genesis 6:9). He didn't get snatched up at the end of his life, but he did get that first-ever cargo-ship ride, which extended his life on earth, as well as his walk with God, for many more years.

Ever since childhood I have looked and listened for this invisible God. The search is different for each of us, but one aspect of it holds true for us all: we want to know we are seen—noticed by our Father. Wouldn't you love to hear God's applause?

Surely we can expect more from our loving Father than a vacant stare. We *can* walk with God in a way that draws His spotlight to our lives and gives us the close connection we're looking for.

Let's take our first step down that path.

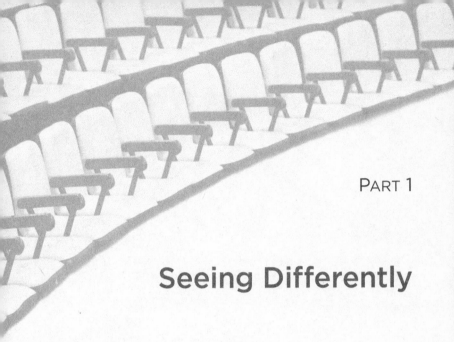

PART 1

Seeing Differently

Walking involves action.

An old Chinese proverb says, "A journey of a thousand miles begins with a single step." There are steps you can take to relate to, and walk with, our invisible God.

Eventually, the steps will involve outward behaviors and practices. But first, we need to practice proper thinking and a form of expanded believing. Without having a biblical perspective of God and how He views us, we'll never experience the rewards and connection He desires for us.

In this section we'll learn to "see" differently. That means seeing biblically, but not boringly.

Compensating for Loss

As a kindergartener I walked from home to school every day after lunch. I felt like a big boy as I ventured off on my twenty-minute journey. After heading out the front door, I'd turn left on the street in front and then take a left down another street. After another left turn and another street, my path finally opened into the school grounds and on to the single-story brick building.

One day as I passed through the giant double doors into the school, something didn't feel right. The lockers lining the walls seemed to stare me down. Big kids (sixth graders) filled the halls and their presence freaked me out more than usual.

Then it hit me. I couldn't hear.

At least not like I was used to hearing. Panic spun me around. I held in my tears until I got back outside the building, then I took off across the playing fields, into the neighborhood, and eventually down my street.

Sprinting into the house, I cried out to Mom, "They're gone!" From the wet tears all over my face, she knew instantly what was the matter.

Mom wrapped me in her arms and explained that everything was okay. Unlike other mornings, she had not inserted my electric "ears" before she sent me out the door. The hearing devices were miniature plastic molds that had to be carefully positioned into my ear canals. They were connected to a clunky receiver resting behind each ear. The batteries needed to be powered up and the settings adjusted just right. It was part of the daily routine of getting little Jeffrey out the door.

But on this particular day, Mom had sent me to school without the electric ears. (They were at the shop for adjustments.) When I arrived at school and noticed the hallway sounds were different, I melted in fear.

Special Ears

Just before I began kindergarten, Mom and Dad learned I had a hearing impairment—about a 60-percent loss in both ears. I was sitting on my dad's lap at the kitchen table one evening while Mom talked on the phone and scribbled on a yellow notepad. When I asked Dad what was going on, he mentioned something about me getting "special ears."

For Mom and Dad, it would involve a crash course on hearing-aid technology, speech therapy, and child-development patterns. They jumped on these issues early, helping me to experience as normal a childhood as possible. Still, there are limits to what parents can do in a situation like this.

When you have a hearing impairment, you make adjustments and relate to the world differently. You learn to read lips—which works wonders when you need to decode what soft-spoken people are saying. You learn to read mannerisms; sometimes a certain look speaks louder than the words you miss. And you learn to enjoy silence too. (Silence is not all bad.)

Of course, when you relate to the world differently, you live differently. When I was in first grade, as soon as the bell would ring for recess, kids would bolt for the playground. But my routine began by stopping at the teacher's desk to remove my "ears," wrap them in a tissue, and put them in a safe place. Then I'd dash outside for a game of kickball. When recess was over, it was back to the teacher's desk to retrieve my ears.

When you can't relate to the world in the same way others do, you experience separation. Life is filled with awkward moments, and it can be a real bummer unless you learn to compensate. Thanks to loving parents who pumped esteem into my bloodstream, I learned to compensate in other areas. Whether it was scoring goals in soccer, winning footraces on the playground, or acing my spelling tests, I was able to find some peace about the thing that set me apart.

Still, I often felt separate from much of what went on around me. Even with my special ears, I missed so much.

Spiritual Separation

Our journey with God is a lot like my journey as a hearing-impaired child. We suffer from separation. We seek a God who does not speak audibly. And we can't see Him with our eyes.

This conflicts with the natural way we develop relationships in life. We get together with friends, we play sports with teammates, we work closely with colleagues, and we come home after work to our family. We enjoy a meal together, look one another in the eye, tell stories, and share experiences.

And then there is God.

Relating to God can feel like having to wear a blindfold at the same time your hearing aids are sent to the shop, then facing the chaos of a crowded school hallway. You are told that God is near and that He is eager to spend time with you. So you do what feels like pushing through crowds, feeling your way in silence down a long hallway, and locating the right door. And then, maybe, God will be in the room you happen to enter.

It's not easy to relate to a God you can't see or hear. We can't see the reaction on His face. We can't feel His touch when we need it. We can't see the look of approval in His eyes.

We also can't see the compassion on His face when He hurts for us.

We can't see His look of concern when we're in danger. And yet we're called not only to believe but also to follow and to actually *love* God with our heart, soul, mind, and strength.

It's tough being separate from God. It's even tougher because we don't know what we're missing. Separation is all we've ever known. Of course, that does not keep us from longing to hear God's applause and to see our Father's delight.

For those who refuse to settle for a life that is disconnected from God, there is hope. Just as I learned to read body language, expressions, and reactions, we can learn to encounter God by hearing, seeing, and living differently. If we learn to compensate, we can see Him even though our physical eyes can't. We can hear Him even though our physical ears don't. We can sense that He is noticing us, even though His face is unseen.

When we relate to God differently, which in this context means biblically, we can have much more of the connection we're looking for.

Choosing Silence

Throughout grade school I continued to tolerate my special ears. When I played football or basketball or soccer, I didn't wear them. In summer when I swam at the neighborhood pool, the hearing aids sat on a desk in my bedroom.

The older I became, the more the look of these gizmos bothered me. I started wearing my hair long enough to cover my ears. By seventh grade, I found ways to minimize the presence of these devices that set me apart from others. Each morning as I stood in front of my locker at school, I did a two-way traffic check. Then I pulled out my ears, slid them into a leather case, and hid them in a pocket.

Sometimes I wore just one of them, usually in the ear that faced the wall when I was seated in a classroom. Eventually I began to leave them both at home. For most of my junior high and high school years, I simply chose not to hear. I chose silence.

My grades remained solid despite my limitations. Still, there were awkward moments. One day in eleventh grade I was reading a literature assignment at my desk and enjoying the sounds of solitude. Suddenly I looked up. The entire class, teacher included, was staring at me. They were talking to me, at me, and about me, desperately trying to get my attention.

I had been oblivious to it all.

Wanting More in Your Walk with God

By the time I left for college, I knew I couldn't go through life choosing this kind of separation, so I put in my special ears and began to reengage. Likewise, we have a choice in applying our spiritual senses to relate to and walk with God. Jesus referred to this as having eyes that see and ears that hear (see Matthew 13:16). We long to see and hear clearly, so why do we often settle for silence? I think it's because we grow used to spiritual separation to the point that living in relative isolation from God seems normal.

But I want more, and I know you do as well. I desire experiences with my heavenly Father like the ones we read about in the Bible—but different. I want personal encounters with God that are just for me.

Occasionally I'll hear a story about someone who had a unique experience with God. Some are simple, straightforward experiences, while others seem outrageous. I don't dismiss anyone's experience with God. It's just that I need my own. And I presume you want to hear and see God in your own life too.

Here is the good news: when it comes to walking more closely with God, a desire for more will work in your favor. You are not the only one who wants more. God does as well.

2

The Comfort of Seeing God's Face

I was in my home office, dialing my cell phone, when the jarring booms of stampeding elephants nearly knocked me out of my chair. Then came screams, more stomping, then louder screams. Things had gotten out of hand upstairs, and it was time to take charge.

Rushing out of my office, I collided with the culprits on the staircase. My red-faced nine-year-old, Gunnar, was crying and coughing, with his hair sticking out in all directions. His two brothers were crowded behind him.

When I demanded answers, all three of my sons blurted out responses. I heard three different stories, but for some reason I trusted the version from the son who had tears on his face. The smirks of his older brothers caused me to doubt their accounts. And when they saw the scowl on my face and smoke coming from my ears, their smiles vanished.

As soon as I heard about how Gunnar's brothers had covered his face with a pillow and sat on top of him so he couldn't breathe, I snapped. In an instant I was transformed into Homer-Simpson-Meets-the-Incredible-Hulk. I ripped into my two older sons, screaming until my voice gave out. (This wasn't holy anger—it was a classic meltdown.) I don't remember what I was shouting, and I'm relieved that no one else was around to hear.

Expecting the All Clear

I returned to my office and pulled out my phone to redial my friend. But there was no need to dial: his name was still displayed on the phone's screen, and the timer was running.

Had I really pocket-dialed a church elder? Yep. He must have heard the entire screaming rant. I thought about hitting the End Call button and maybe moving to another state. I had come unglued and lost my cool while someone I respected listened in. Thankfully, I have a track record with this man.

I took a deep breath and said, "I guess you heard all that, huh?" He had. But he had also raised three sons of his own and seemed to understand. (Plus, now he had a great story to tell his wife.)

After the call, and once the color in my face had returned to normal, my thoughts shifted. *What if I had glanced at my phone and seen God's name on the display?*

Instead of thinking about a church leader hearing my rant, I began to think about God watching me scream at my kids. After all, I have God pocket-dialed every moment of every day.

A Father's View

The thought of God standing nearby and listening in on our daily lives can bring comfort…or terror. It can evoke shame, or it can connect with the part of us that wants to please our Father. How we deal with this reality will shape our walk with God. It all depends on our perspective of God's face.

When I glanced at my phone and saw my friend's name, my heart sank. What an embarrassment. But when I began to think instead about God watching me, in a strange but real way that made me feel better.

This may sound backward. But in these moments I am reminded that God sees me all the time. He knows my every waking thought. While I regret my behavior at times, thankfully I can recover more easily with God than I can with others. God knows me completely—nothing about me surprises Him.

Some may view God as one who pops in and out of view, catching us off guard, somewhat like my pocket-dialing experience. If you believe this perspective, it will cause you to keep looking over your shoulder, wondering what God might be thinking about you.

Others assume God pays attention only when we mess up—as if life is a highly dysfunctional game of hide-and-seek. I can't think of a more oppressive way to live.

It's easy to think God is put off by our flaws and mistakes. In situations where we don't measure up, even to our own standards, we might assume that God's countenance shifts immediately from a smile to a frown. Some may even picture God turning away from us or reaching for something He can use to punish us. If this were true of God, we'd be justified in wanting to keep our distance.

But the reality that God is watching speaks of His care. His watchful ways are intended to inspire, not frighten us. This is one of the key mind shifts necessary to hearing God's applause. It all has to do with how you picture God's face.

Face Time with God

In the Garden of Eden, Adam and Eve had a daily Visitor who walked around and spent time with them: God. Between visits, He was watching them. How amazing would it be to have those walk-and-talk sessions today, to see God's face up close and hear His voice?

When God expressed pleasure toward Abel and the gift he brought, it was clear to both Abel and his brother, Cain, how God felt. Cain also had brought a gift, and the difference in God's reaction was apparent. God saw the two boys and their gifts differently, and Cain didn't know how to handle it.

I wonder how Cain understood God's feelings. Did God speak from the clouds, or did He walk up and speak to the brothers face to face? If it was a direct encounter, did God's facial expression change when He looked from Abel to Cain? Maybe Abel's face lit up because he saw the delight on God's face.

We don't know how quickly face time with God diminished after Adam and Eve were banished from the garden. We know that eventually, the separation between God and the people He created caused the common experience of face-to-face walking with God to disappear. God was no longer visible to His children.

At some point, it became dangerous to try to see God's face. Encountering His glory was too much for an earthly being to survive. When Moses met with God on the mountain, he didn't see God's face, but he did get close. (God covered Moses with His hand to protect him.) Whatever Moses saw caused his face to shine like a floodlight. When he returned from the mountain and the people saw his glow, they were alarmed. But soon they saw that he was safe—and learned that he had had an encounter with the living God.

Having God's attention was to their benefit. God told the people through Moses: "the LORD make his *face* shine upon you and be gracious to you; the LORD turn his *face* toward you and give you peace" (Numbers 6:25–26).

God's children sought comfort from the sight of God's face. Notice the words of King David: "Let the light of your *face* shine upon us" (Psalm 4:6). And again: "My heart says of you, 'Seek his *face*!' Your *face*, LORD, I will seek" (Psalm 27:8). The thought of seeing God's face was not frightening to David. He longed to see the face of God. He relished the idea that God was watching him.

God has His eyes fixed on you too, which always is in your favor. In the chapters that follow, we will explore what it means that the Father turns His eyes toward us. You won't be rattled by the idea that God is watching you. God pays close attention to each of us, which should be a source of comfort and confidence. He does not keep watch so He can catch you in a pocket-dial. He's watching because He's interested in you.

3

God Is Interested

I stood on the first tee box, looking down the fairway toward the flag nearly four hundred yards away. I was sixteen, and this was one of my few junior golf tournaments. Compared to my regular golfing buddies, I was an average player. But when I entered tournament play, where the real golfers hung out, I usually posted among the worst scores—if not *the* worst—in the field.

I loved the sport, and Dad encouraged me to sign up for tournaments. Registration came with a free lunch, several rounds of golf, a sleeve of fresh balls, and a bag of goodies to litter the pockets of my golf bag. Since I didn't play many tournaments, each one felt like a first. That day, standing nervously among the players in my group, I knew there was a good chance I might shank the ball into the driving range off to the right, as I'd done many times before.

In the past when that happened, I'd pull out another ball and pretend the first shot never happened. But I wouldn't be doing that today—this was serious play. A duffed shot would be more costly: a few extra strokes reflected on the scorecard, blown confidence to start the round, and a reminder to me that maybe I didn't belong here.

It was important to get the first shot in the clear.

While awaiting my turn, I studied the other players in my group. Everything about them showed they had more experience playing the game. Their clubs, their bags, their shoes, the swings they took, their confident swaggers. Plus, they seemed to already know one another from the summer golf circuit. I was the outsider.

Unfortunately, since my last name starts with an A, I often was assigned to the first group. My name, of all things, guaranteed extra butterflies.

When it was my turn to tee off, I happened to glance behind me toward the clubhouse. A figure standing alone behind the starter box caught my eye. Squinting, I saw him more clearly. He was standing in his dark suit watching the action from a distance, trying not to be seen.

It was Dad.

I gave a slight nod. We both knew no greeting was necessary. None of the other dads were around, just mine. These tournaments were not the kind to draw a gallery, but Dad wanted to catch my first swing before heading to the office.

I realize now that no matter where I was, Dad often was watching. He was interested in everything I did.

Home-Court Advantage

I had a definite advantage in life. I had parents who loved me, who were a stable force in my life. And they were always watching. They were not there to make sure I didn't mess up—no, they were watching because of a connection, a deep love. That's what helped me to live with confidence.

When I was a small child, I often crawled out of bed in the middle of the night to go to the bathroom. Even when I tried to be quiet, as soon as I'd tiptoe into the hall, Dad would be there to turn on the bathroom light. He'd wait for me, then tuck me back into bed. I wondered if all dads had Superman ears—or if it was just my dad. I'm sure my weak hearing made my dad's hearing seem that much more "super."

My mom tells me that when I would leave the house after lunch, headed to kindergarten, she always followed me with her eyes. I would turn the first corner and disappear from view. She knew how long it should take me to enter the open field. Looking out across our backyard, she would watch for me to reappear at just the right time.

As a Little League baseball player approaching the plate to bat, I'd nonchalantly glance behind me to see that Mom and Dad were watching. They were always easy to spot in the bleachers. So a few years later when I got ready to tee off in a junior golf tournament and I saw Dad from a distance, it wasn't a huge surprise. That was life for Jeff Anderson: my father was watching.

Eyes from Above

This parenting style shaped my view of God in massive ways. It also has guided me in how I understand the Scriptures. For instance, it makes sense to me when the apostle Paul refers to us as "God's children" who cry, "*Abba,* Father!" (Romans 8:15–16).

When I read about God's eyes scanning the earth (see 2 Chronicles 16:9), I have a vivid image of God watching over me in protective ways, just as my earthly father did when I was a child.

When Jesus reminds us of the First Commandment, to love God, it's not a huge stretch for me to understand God as a loving Father who inspires love in His children. God's presence serves as a comforting shadow to me, much like that of my earthly father taking time to watch me do battle on the fairways.

I'm reminded of Nathanael just before he was selected to be one of the twelve disciples. Nathanael did not know Jesus, but Jesus knew him. " 'How do you know me?' Nathanael asked. Jesus answered, 'I *saw* you while you were still under the fig tree before Philip called you' " (John 1:48).

Immediately Nathanael recognized Jesus as the Son of God (see John 1:49). Nathanael knew God's eyes were on him and that, evidently, God was pleased with what He saw.

Sadly Unique

I realize many people did not grow up in a stable, loving family. I was in college when I first became aware of the pain that young men carried with them from childhood. I lived in a fraternity house where cool confidence was tattooed on faces. But deep inside were fragile minds and fractured perspectives, distorted by father experiences far different from mine.

Whether you share my experience or a less favorable one, I challenge you to view God as your Father who delights in you as His child. God is accessible, approachable...and He is waiting to engage with you. Getting a right perspective of God affects far more than just how you approach Him. It determines the way you live in every area of your life.

If you picture God frowning at you, the Christian journey will be difficult. If you sense God is always looking away from you, trying to find someone who is more interesting, you will never take Him seriously. But if your God is One who is always there, always interested, always finding pleasure in you as His child, you will have eyes that see Him in very relatable ways.

And you will learn to trust Him enough to try seemingly unreasonable things to connect at a deeper level.

The Necessity of Taking a Risk

Many summers after my junior-golf experiences, I was back on the links with a college diploma and a job offer in hand. Dad had sold me on the idea of deferring my employment until September. I would live at home for a few months, study for the CPA exam, and play lots of golf. So, of course, that's what I did.

A big change from previous summers was that my friends were now at work. When I showed up at the golf course alone, I paired with businesspeople taking a vacation day or retired guys wearing the latest in last century's golf fashion.

Being a young buck eager to conquer the world, I made it a habit to ask my playing partners, "What advice do you have for me? What would you do differently if you were my age again?"

A few answered with a life story. Others answered with a few short sentences. Some were seasoned business leaders with impressive stories to share. Others had fewer life trophies on the shelf.

Regardless of age or life experience, however, there was a clear consensus: take risks. Often, they had followed the easier path and now regretted not having taken a chance. It may have been a business venture, a different path in education, an investment opportunity, a career detour, a relationship risk.

That summer I made a clearheaded decision: I would become a risk taker.

Life Risks and Faith Risks

I had just completed a four-year degree in one of the most risk-averse fields—accounting! But my golf partners passed along more life lessons than I could ever have learned in bean-counting school.

I started a job in the fall and business travel took me to Las Vegas, where I was introduced to blackjack. I'd heard about some professionals who made a nice living playing the game and learning how to set up the dealer with a busted hand. I found that playing this card game was way more enjoyable than auditing a corporation's books, so I began to ponder ways to make a career of playing blackjack.

Somehow wisdom got in the way, and I kept my day job. But five years later, I left accounting to become a stock day-trader. At the time I had a bride of nearly two years and a nine-month-old baby, so leaving a secure job was a gamble.

When I tendered my resignation, my boss questioned my decision. But his skepticism made it feel all the more right. My former golf sages would be proud! Leaving a steady paycheck for the uncertainty of making money on the stock market was a measured risk.

But I took a far bigger risk when I decided to take my faith more seriously.

I had grown up in the church and had done the churchy things. I attended regularly, carried around my Bible, mastered the trivia and the sword drills, tithed 10 percent, and said my prayers. But along the way it occurred to me (code for "hearing God's whisper") that I wasn't taking risks…at least not the ones that would help my walk with God.

When I came across folks who were taking faith risks, their behavior always stood out. Not necessarily their words, but certain choices they made. The more their faith got my attention, the more I sensed it was getting God's attention too. He cares about these things.

The risk takers seemed to hear God in ways that I didn't. They seemed to take the teachings of Jesus more literally than I did. And they seemed to enjoy particular rewards that I wasn't experiencing.

I realized (okay, it was another Spirit nudge) that even though I knew God was watching me, I hadn't given Him much to watch. I wasn't taking risks with my faith, and I wasn't seeing rewards either. God was watching as I stood on life's tee box. But I wasn't taking a big swing with the club.

A Starting Point

Taking risks is not easy. Risks involve uncertainties, and who likes that? But as you've likely heard said, without risks there can be no rewards. And when it comes to our walk with God, rewards (deeper connections) are what we're after.

Taking risks begins with trying on a new perspective. You might need to reshape how you view God as your Father. If you've never imagined God watching you, finding delight in you, we're going to frame that view in more detail.

For others, perhaps you see God's fatherly presence clearly, but you feel like a spectator, as I did. If so, it's time to step into new experiences that will get His attention.

Instead of wondering what the Bible says about this and that, we're going to explore what happens when you *act* on what the Bible says and then experience the rewards that follow.

You can't move forward with God without moving. Together we are going to engage our faith and chase the heart of the living God. Consider this your starting point to start moving, to begin taking risks. Today.

We all need personal proof of God's presence. I'm learning that God enjoys personal proof of *our* presence!

The faith adventure is a test of endurance. A lifetime of following an invisible God is not easy. It's natural to want to know God is real—not someday after we die, but now, right here, right next to us.

Let me assure you, He is real. And it's His heart's desire to reveal Himself to you in everyday life and in ordinary situations. Let's see what that looks like.

4

Creating Secrets with God

When Stephanie and I began dating, the relationship moved at warp speed, driven by good looks (hers) and deep conversation (a team effort). We trusted each other with our most treasured thought-gems, our dreams and successes, insecurities and failures. The more we revealed our secrets, the deeper our bond grew.

As Stephanie unpacked her childhood wounds—she lost her mother to cancer—her feelings merged with mine. When I shared my personal dreams for the future, she allowed them to merge with hers.

Talk quickly turned to marriage. We plotted a course that would involve two job changes and a move to another state. And as big as all this was, we kept our plans to ourselves. When friends would ask how things were going, we might give a simple answer, then move on to another subject. Meanwhile, Stephanie and I would glance at each other and smile. We knew big things were ahead.

We cherished our secrets.

A wedding followed (yes, we did finally share) and so did new jobs and an out-of-state move. Before we celebrated our six-month anniversary, Stephanie had become pregnant. After the initial shock of realizing we were about to become parents, we embraced the good news. But we waited more than four months before breaking the news even to our families. Stephanie and I had that kind of connection. We treasured our secrets.

When you have a deepening walk with someone you love, secrets take on a meaning that goes beyond shared knowledge. The longer you savor the secrets, the deeper the bond penetrates the heart and soul of a relationship.

If you've ever shared a close relationship with a spouse, child, or a best friend, you know what I'm talking about. Now, here's the kicker: the special bond that comes from creating, sharing, and keeping secrets is not reserved for human relationships. God wants in on the action too.

God enjoys having secrets that are exclusive between the two of you.

A Test of Friendship

Picture this. You are the disciple James. (I picked James because he doesn't get enough press.) Jesus asks you to join him, Peter, and your brother John on a hike up a mountain.

Nothing unusual takes place as you trudge to the top. But then you see your Teacher transformed into a glowing figure brighter than a flash of lightning. And, oh yeah: He is talking with Moses and Elijah!

As you walk back down the mountain, Jesus asks you to keep a secret. "Don't tell anyone what you have seen" (Matthew 17:9).

Are you kidding me? You saw your Rabbi slip on a heaven costume and step out of time to converse with the leading prophets of Israel. And He expects you not to say anything about it?

You, Jesus, and the two other hikers return to the disciples who were not invited along. Oddly enough, the left-behind disciples start asking Jesus questions about, you guessed it, Elijah. Can you imagine that moment? There had to be glances and grins exchanged among Peter, John, and you—and Jesus. It was like the four of you were saying, *As a matter of fact, we were just chatting with Elijah! And by the way, Moses says to tell you guys "Hello."*

But you would never say these things out loud. Jesus told you to keep this amazing encounter a secret.

Why Not Us?

Why didn't Jesus take all twelve of His closest disciples on that trek, instead of just three? Perhaps the relationship with the other nine, although solid, had not yet grown to the love and trust level of creating and keeping secrets. Or maybe He simply wanted to experience something deeper with the three who were invited along.

Whatever the case, Jesus fostered secrets to honor and deepen key relationships. Some information He shared with the crowds; some He reserved for the twelve disciples; and some He told only to His closest three followers.

Often, after teaching parables to the masses, Jesus had a follow-up session with His disciples to explain His teachings and to answer their questions. In the days leading up to His death, resurrection, and ascension, He shared mysterious secrets with the Twelve. He spoke to them as friends (see John 15:15).

Jesus knew they would need extra attention and encouragement to carry out the Great Commission after His departure. And the relational tool He used to solidify and deepen these relationships was the sharing of secrets.

Secret Ingredients

Stephanie and I both contribute to building our marriage relationship. We invest time and emotional energy into each other's lives. Our shared involvement frees us to communicate what's on our hearts. As a result, we trust each other more deeply. We are able to connect at times without spoken words.

That's how meaningful relationships blossom.

When it comes to your relationship with God, you and He both have a part to play. God is interested in your full engagement—the investment of your emotional energy—into a relationship with Him. In return, He is prepared to respond to you.

So how does it work that we can share secrets with our Father? What leads to this depth of sharing? For starters, let's look at a sermon in which Jesus talked about secrets.

In Matthew 6, Jesus specified three spiritual practices that are to be done in secret. He said, "So when you give.... When you pray.... When you fast" (verses 2, 5, 16). These three were not chosen at random. They are significant themes in Jesus's teachings and throughout Scripture. But sermons about giving, praying, and fasting don't necessarily draw big crowds today.

I understand why. A sermon on giving makes people nervous. Add prayer (which makes people sleepy) and fasting (listeners assume it applies to others, not to them), then see who comes back next week. In spite of all this, Jesus lumped them all together and after a hit-and-run mention of each, He circled back to the theme of giving.

Why did He place so much emphasis on these three practices? For starters, each one involves giving up something we need, or think we need, to live comfortably.

Giving away our money costs us financially. It could mean having to do without luxuries or even basics.

Praying costs us in time, sleep, and emotional energy. And it likely will mean taking on the burdens, needs, and hurts of others.

Fasting costs us physically by testing our comfort zone. Who likes being hungry or feeling weak or lightheaded from skipping meals?

Each of these practices costs us personally. When you reach out to God in these ways, He notices, and you have a golden opportunity to create a secret. And secrets build relationships.

Jesus made it clear that giving, prayer, and fasting are best practiced as secrets. (They can accurately be called *secret ingredients*.) Jesus instructed His followers to do these things privately. The point of it all is not simply to have secrets—but that sharing secrets with God brings reward: "Your Father, who sees what is done in secret, will *reward* you" (Matthew 6:4, 6, 18).

Jesus uses this expression three times—maybe so hard-of-hearing folks like me will get it. God sees what we do in secret, He notices, and He rewards us. That connection should wake us up. Jesus was not just giving us a task list. Rather, this is a personal invitation for you to enter into closeness with your Father and then to enjoy His rewards.

Jesus mentions the rewards seven times in the short Secret Sermon. Often He is referring to heavenly rewards—applause from God that we won't experience until "tomorrow." These rewards will remind us later how much God noticed us back on earth.

But some of the rewards are experienced today. These are simple nudges—encounters with God—that help us see what we all are longing to know: that God sees us now, in this life. We don't have to wait until we enter heaven to know we have His attention.

The Secret Sermon

Be careful not to do your "acts of righteousness" before men, to be seen by them. If you do, you will have no *reward* from your Father in heaven.

So when you give to the needy, do not announce it with trumpets, as the hypocrites do in the synagogues and on the streets, to be honored by men. I tell you the truth, they have received their *reward* in full. But when you give to the needy, do not let your left hand know what your right hand is doing, so that your giving may be in *secret*. Then your Father, who sees what is done in *secret*, will *reward* you.

And when you pray, do not be like the hypocrites, for they love to pray standing in the synagogues and on the street corners to be seen by men. I tell you the truth, they have received their *reward* in full. But when you pray, go into your room, close the door and pray to your Father, who is unseen. Then your Father, who sees what is done in *secret*, will *reward* you. And when you pray, do not keep on babbling like pagans, for they think they will be heard because of their many words. Do not be like them, for your Father knows what you need before you ask him....

When you fast, do not look somber as the hypocrites do, for they disfigure their faces to show men they are fasting. I tell you the truth, they have received their *reward* in full. But when you fast, put oil on your head and wash your face, so that it will not be obvious to men that you are fasting, but only to your Father, who is unseen; and your Father, who sees what is done in *secret*, will *reward* you. (Matthew 6:1–8, 16–18)

Focused on Our Invisible Father

When I was dating Stephanie and I gave her special gifts or affirmed her with my words, I always looked straight into her eyes. I sought a direct connection that went beyond speaking words or handing her a token of my love. When we were not together—if we were talking on the phone or if I was writing her a note—I pictured her face.

God wants us to be focused on Him in similar ways. When we give, pray, and fast, our eyes should be squarely on our Father, as if He were in front of us. Of course, God is invisible. That's why these practices involve faith.

At mealtime with my family, if one of us tosses up a hurried, token prayer of thanks, I'll sometimes stop things midprayer. I'll ask, "Is this prayer for God or for us? If it's for us, I guess a rushed 'thank you' will do. If it's for God, we should start over."

A time-out can remind us God is listening. We're praying to God, our Father, and not just talking to other family members sitting at the table, hungry for dinner. This type of mindfulness can shake us out of a pattern of "vain repetitions" (see Matthew 6:7, NKJV), which Jesus warned against. Stopping to reflect on God's watchfulness helps us to discover new experiences through familiar activities such as prayer.

Toil in the Garden

At our house, when I look out my office window, I see a garden. My wife loves her garden (keyword *her*). One way that I have learned to love Stephanie is to appreciate the hours she spends digging in the dirt. She goes through ridiculous pains, from my perspective, to plant vegetables in buckets and wire cages to keep moles and gophers from pulling out the roots.

Come springtime, she'll get our boys out to prepare the soil for planting. When I see one of my sons on hands and knees in the dirt, wiping his sweaty brow with a forearm, it touches my heart. But other times, when I see one of my sons wearing headphones, lost in a separate world, kicking the planter buckets and shirking work like a sluggard, my heart is not moved at all.

Likewise, there is something about sacrifice that gets our Father's attention.

When we give, pray, fast, or do anything else that is directed toward Him in ways that cost us, God notices. He smiles and rewards us. And if we pay attention, we can hear His applause.

When the widow came to the Temple to sacrifice her two mites, Jesus noticed. When Zacchaeus sacrificed half his possessions to give to the poor, Jesus noticed. When Mary cracked open a bottle of perfume worth a year's wages to anoint the head and feet of Jesus, He noticed and praised her.

In these cases and others, Jesus made a big deal about the actions taken. He celebrated their acts by calling attention to them.

Secrets or Sacrifice

You've heard the expressions *sacrificial giving* and *give till it hurts.* The intent behind these phrases can be positive, but they are easily misunderstood. If you try giving till it hurts (whatever that means to you) but you don't believe God is watching with pleasure, it *will* hurt. But if you give secretly and know that God sees you, the experience will be very different.

God sees your sacrifice. Your job is to be focused so you will *see* God, who sees your sacrifice. When you believe God is watching, sacrifice makes sense (and so does giving in secret). If you don't really believe God is watching, sacrifice is just sacrifice. Instead of connecting with God through the shared secret, you'll seek a connection with other people by mentioning your sacrifice. (Need proof? Just log on to Facebook.)

Jesus said whenever you sacrifice in order to draw attention to yourself, you forfeit the reward from God (see Matthew 6:2, 5, 16). Whatever attention you would have received from God is transferred to the attention you receive from others. This is a great way to cheat yourself.

Philanthropists, celebrities, and garden-variety Christians who like to see their names added to a list of gold- or silver-level contributors don't have to worry about God's view of their sacrifices. They can enjoy the worldly recognition of being praised for their generous support of a cause. Hopefully they choose their causes well; otherwise, what a waste.

But for those who give (or pray or fast or serve) with their focus on God, His attention alone is more than enough reward.

Close Encounters

As you connect with God through secret giving, prayer, and fasting, you can expect to have encounters with God. He has seen you, and you should now watch for Him.

We read about figures in the Bible who were noticed by God after secret acts:

- Solomon offered burnt offerings; God visited Him in a dream (see 1 Kings 3:4–5).
- Cornelius offered prayers to God and gave gifts to the poor; God set up an appointment with an angel (see Acts 10:2–3).
- Moses fasted for forty days; God met him on a mountain and gave him tablets containing the Ten Commandments inscribed by the finger of God (see Deuteronomy 9:9–10).

When you get God's attention, He will get yours.

Some encounters with the Spirit of God are extraordinary. Whenever they happen, we should let them soak into our hearts.

Consider the story of Samson, who was traveling with his parents when a lion charged him. The Spirit of the Lord came on Samson, who then tore the lion to pieces. It was an explosive encounter with the power of God, and Samson knew it. But somehow his parents missed the scene. (How is it they didn't hear all the growling and grunting?) Think about Samson, who had just saved his parents' lives. He must have been tempted to mention his feat of bravery, but he didn't say anything (see Judges 14:6). He knew that what was happening between God and him was special—something to be kept secret between them.

When Saul was made Israel's first king, the Spirit of God came upon him and he prophesied with other prophets (see 1 Samuel 10:10). But when he approached his uncle, Saul did not even mention that he had been chosen as Israel's king (see 1 Samuel 10:16). He deflected attention to some lost donkeys instead.

Perhaps no one else mastered the gift of secrets like the mother of Jesus did. An angel told Mary that the Christ child would be conceived inside her by the power of God's Spirit. After Jesus was born, the angels appeared, and word began to spread about this mysterious child. But "Mary treasured up all these things and pondered them in her heart" (Luke 2:19). Can you imagine being entrusted with that kind of news—that the Savior of the world was your very own child?

Twelve years later, when the boy Jesus was discovered deep in discussion with the religious teachers and experts in the Law, Mary treasured even more closely held secrets (see Luke 2:51). Are there any proud mamas out there who think it would be difficult to keep such a secret?

As we will see in the chapters that follow, the rewards of secret encounters with God are exhilarating. They remind you that God really does see you. Such encounters warrant your reverent care and attention.

Guard them closely as the special secrets they are. Call them to mind as you walk with your invisible—but very present—God.

Do You Keep Secrets with God?

Have you ever questioned why your relationship with God doesn't feel more real?

If you are honest about it, you might admit that you have written off the possibility of experiencing something more authentic. Or it could be that you have not taken the step of creating secrets with your Father.

Social media, shortened attention spans, and a culture that bombards us with input make it difficult to keep anything to ourselves. Check out these social-media posts:

- I just prayed twenty straight minutes for everyone I can think of. Wow, that felt great! Hold on, you guys, help is on the way.
- Just had two divine appointments back to back... What a day!
- All-night prayer session at church...feeling refreshed.
- Woke up at 3:45 this morning to pray with someone before he heads to the hospital for surgery. I'm living on coffee.

Jesus meant what He said about secrets and rewards in Matthew 6. It applies as much today as it did two thousand years ago. Secrets are worth keeping. Secrets build relationships.

Consider the night when the angel Gabriel visited Mary. Can you imagine Mary posting on Facebook, "My Son will bear the sins of the world"? Or maybe with a bumper sticker that says "My Son will save your son's soul?" I don't think so. We are told that she pondered these secrets in her heart.

I'm not trying to trash social media. But we should examine the balance of time, energy, and heart we devote to posting personal data to the world, and the time, energy, and heart we devote to nurturing our private thoughts with God.

God desires to share secrets with you—*just for you*.

Course Correction

When we squander opportunities for secrets, we squander the chance to relish the moment with God. He may have something more in store for us. But we time-out its value by choosing instead the cheap attention of others.

In a dream, Joseph had a personal encounter with God. Rather than privately treasuring the secret (a special prophecy) from God, he boasted about it to his brothers. They were not impressed, and Joseph later found himself tossed into a pit, then sold into slavery (see Genesis 37).

Samson had supernatural strength, thanks to his good hair. Initially, he did well to keep his secrets. (Remember the lion he took on bare-handed?) But at some point he became careless. When he shared the secret of his divine strength with a not-so-nice girlfriend, he woke up with a really bad haircut (see Judges 16). It was more than awkward—it was a deadly game changer.

Violating a secret does not always trigger that magnitude of destruction. Still, the principle is that when we divulge the secrets we have with God it can damage the connection He wants to have with us.

If I had spoken loosely of the secrets my wife shared during our engagement, it would have set our relationship back. If she had given a play-by-play commentary of my secrets to her friends, it would have crushed me and weakened my trust in her. Secret encounters are like layers of superglue that bond hearts tightly together.

Let's create, and treasure, secrets with God. Let's accept the truth that there are deeper rewards ahead, rewards not worth trading for quick attention from others.

But Didn't Jesus Say...?

Just before He preached the Secret Sermon, Jesus said to the crowds, "You are the light of the world.... Let your light shine before men, that they may see your good deeds and praise your Father in heaven" (Matthew 5:14, 16). I know, it sounds like double-talk. What do we make of these paradoxical commands of hiding in a prayer closet while shining a light to the world?

When Jesus mentioned giving, praying, and fasting in secret, He did not say you should never be seen. He simply said not to do these things *to be seen,* or for the purpose of being seen (see Matthew 6:1). There's a difference.

Walking with God involves making new disciples who also walk with God and who teach others to walk with God. Making disciples involves training, and the deeper lessons we have learned through our own secrets with God make for an effective textbook for teaching others.

Jesus shared secret experiences with the disciples to help develop them as leaders. Paul shared some of his stories, helping new believers to follow in his footsteps.

There were times when Jesus would heal people or send off new converts with an instruction to go and share their new experience with their family and friends. Both seasoned disciple makers and new learners can benefit from sharing certain fresh experiences with others.

Don't Sweat the Rules

Part of a walk with God is learning the ebb and flow of when secrets should remain secret and when they can be helpful to others. Of course, if you're married, sharing secrets as a couple is necessary to grow together in your walk with God. And often God will lead you to spiritual mentors who help you to process your journey. Sharing secrets with them can be healthy too.

Maybe you've bottled up your secrets for a long time, and God is nudging you to share. Maybe a teaching opportunity comes your way or a discipleship assignment or chance to share a story. At those times it's appropriate to share.

Determining when to share a secret and when to keep it is not a science, but an art. Trial and error is part of the process. Looking up to God—and not exclusively to others—will help you know when and how to share your secrets.

After Joseph spilled the beans on his earlier secret (the prophetic dream), he mastered the skill of keeping secrets. Many years later, Joseph encountered his brothers again. This time he displayed keen wisdom and foresight in managing his secrets, setting up a most awestruck family reunion for his father, Jacob.

Joseph learned that secrets are worth keeping and that they often build toward big, life-changing encounters with God.

Love and Secrets

You know what really spurs on secrets between Stephanie and me? Love. It's easier to understand the power of secrets when you love someone.

As you and I journey together, I trust that something else will start to make a lot more sense to you: loving God. The Great Commandment is about loving God with all our being, including our heart, mind, and strength. But loving God can be a fuzzy concept. Really, how are you supposed to love God in this all-encompassing way? And it doesn't help that God is invisible to our physical eyes. It's hard to love someone when you're not certain He notices you.

Loving God goes hand in hand with learning to notice that He is noticing you. As you do the things that get God's attention, you find the relationship becomes more real. Secrets begin to flow. Special encounters follow, and your connection to God deepens. Suddenly, loving God with your whole heart makes a lot more sense.

And even though God remains invisible, you realize He's not distant. You connect with Him while driving to or from work, while completing a project, while mowing the lawn or weeding the garden.

Or even while watching a youth basketball game.

5

A Buzzer Shot from God

If you ever need some comic relief, youth basketball is sure to deliver. I'm surprised it's not featured on ESPN—or Comedy Central.

Most eight-year-olds aren't ready for the demands of the game. The kid-sized ball feels like a pumpkin to them. Dribbling is a two-handed exercise for most. *Traveling* (walking with the ball) is illegal but rarely draws a whistle. Guarding the opponent looks more like bear hugs and slaps.

When the game becomes too much of a contact sport, a whistle sounds and the wronged player takes a foul shot. But foul shots are useless. They drain nearly a minute off a clock that never stops, and most free throws never go near the rim. It's difficult to rack up points. A final score may be ten to six, with all-star teams putting a few dozen points on the scoreboard.

Watching from the Stands

I was perched in the stands on a Saturday morning, watching Gunnar's last game of the season. The clock was winding down to the final seconds, which means parents were shuffling into the gym for the next game while others were heading out.

The two teams on the floor were among the league's strongest, and this final game was an epic battle. The score was eighteen to nineteen. We were down by a point with eighteen seconds on the clock. In college hoops, eighteen seconds is enough time for several timeouts, some well-planned fouls, and a few TV breaks—maybe five to ten minutes of basketball. But with these little fellas, eighteen seconds meant it was time for parents to stand up, grab jackets and toddlers, and get ready to head to the parking lot.

Gunnar's team had possession so his coach called a final time-out. The players huddled around him as he drew up a desperation play. For a youth basketball coach, drawing up any kind of play is a shot in the dark. Things rarely go as planned with ten miniature athletes on the court. But it's worth a try.

As we waited, I had an inexplicable God-connection moment. In my most silent of conversations (in my heart and mind), I threw out a crazy scenario. *God, if Gunnar should happen to have the ball in the final seconds, that would really be something. And if he should get off the final shot, that would be something too…*

And if the shot should go in the basket, causing our team to win the game, I'll take it as a hook shot from heaven.

There were plenty of *ifs* in that equation. So many, in fact, that if Gunnar were to get the ball, put up a shot, and make the basket, it would make a statement that I couldn't overlook. This was not a "Please make this happen" prayer or even a wish. This had nothing to do with my trying to enlist God on the side of my son's team. And it wasn't about Gunnar's being a hero, although every kid treasures the thought of making a last-second shot.

This was just about God and me. It was a moment for us to connect and for me to be reminded of what I already knew: God sees me. I know that to be true just like I know my name, but still it's great to have some reminders. If I saw these secret *ifs* take place on the court, I would receive it as a message from God.

I went over the *ifs* a few times in my head, then took a deep breath. No longer was this about children in a gym playing youth basketball. It was about a grown man sitting in the stands, asking God, *Do you see me?*

Taking a Risky Shot

The referee blew his whistle to signal the end of the timeout. One more whistle, then the ball was back in play. After two quick passes, the ball was in Gunnar's hands. He dribbled past the half-court line and dished it off to the designated playmaker.

Immediately, the teammate dribbled the ball to the baseline, where he was greeted with bear hugs and body slaps from a player on the other team. But this was no time for another whistle, so the refs let the kids play. The setup routine was chewing up the clock. Finally, the playmaker put up a shot.

Like most shots taken by these pint-sized players, the ball sailed over the rim and descended to the other side. At least a dozen little arms reached for the ball. One of our players caught it and scooted toward the basket (scooting is allowed for eight-year-olds). The clock was ticking, and the yelling from all directions grew in volume and intensity.

The rebounder launched the ball straight up in the air, and it fell straight down. The clock was almost to zero.

Gunnar caught the descending pumpkin and immediately launched it back into the air. Just as the ball left his hands, the buzzer sounded. The action on the court seemed to freeze. The noisy crowd turned silent as the ball hung in the air. Just like in the movies. Finally, it began its decent and fell to the floor. But not without first dropping through the rim.

"Nothin' but net," as they say.

The crowd erupted. The stands emptied (time to go home). The opposing team's bewildered coach fell to the floor and lay on his back like a snow angel. The grin on his face was his admission that luck—or something like it—was surely in the air.

The players on the losing team were shedding tears. Eight-year-olds don't usually cry, but the suspense and last-second reversal of winners and losers was a little too much.

Our coach's wife ran from the stands to give Gunnar a hug. His victorious teammates huddled around him. Within seconds, I was alone in the stands. I gathered up the coats and made my way to the court.

The players were ecstatic and so were the parents. Gunnar was happy. It's fun to be the hero.

I was feeling something quite different. Sure, I was proud of my son and happy for the team. But it really wasn't about the shot or the victory. Our family had experienced plenty of losses in youth sports, and those Saturdays always turned out fine.

On this day, following the buzzer-shot victory, I was caught up in something bigger. I had connected with God. I had taken a risk, a shot of my own. And my Father had connected with me. God winked at me, and I couldn't help but worship Him in my heart. No one knew it, though. It was a private moment.

Personal Encounters with God

I know this God encounter is a far cry from the Transfiguration witnessed by the three disciples. Or Joseph encountering his brothers who had sold him into slavery more than a decade earlier. If you think mine is a strange story, I can understand why. The buzzer shot doesn't match the personal encounters of Solomon's conversation with God in a dream or Mary's being visited by an angel.

But it *was* a special encounter…just between God and me.

Sure, I was nestled in the comfort of a warm gym on a cold winter day, while millions of people struggled with real problems and faced real needs. So why would I waste God's time with my silly request?

It wasn't a waste of His time. Clearly He chose to let me know that *He saw me.* I was noticed by my Father. Of course my buzzer-shot request did not crowd out the more important world affairs from God's view. Yet in the midst of attending to the big needs, God also pays attention to things such as buzzer-shot prayers and the trajectory of a basketball in a high school gym.

God is more engaged with us than we realize. He has more bandwidth than we can imagine. He's listening, He's watching, and He's waiting.

Don't we all long to see God's hand at work, to hear Him voice His approval, to feel His touch? Don't we hope for interactions with God to connect with Him in simple ways?

God is not a genie. And answering a buzzer-shot prayer is not a magic trick He performs for our personal entertainment. God does not wait for us to snap our fingers before He puts in an appearance. But in special moments, when we're after something deeper, God wants to connect with us.

Buzzer-shot connections are special and can be infrequent. Solomon encountered the Lord in a dream, and twenty years passed before he had a second visit from God. Such encounters whet our appetite for more, and they hold us over during seasons of silence.

Sometimes these encounters propel life forward in miraculous ways. The angel's message to Mary was a game changer for her and for the world! Other times they influence seemingly trivial matters, such as an eight-year-old tossing a basketball and seeing it drop through the hoop.

The unfortunate thing is that too many of us never seek out such a moment of connection with our Father. It's as if we assume God has a limited attention span, so we don't seek His attention. Or worse, we feel that He simply doesn't care about our needs and concerns.

A Life That Gets God's Attention

God's hook shot from heaven got *my* attention, but perhaps what happened is that I got *His* attention first. Often we're looking for a signal from God, but it could be that He's looking for a signal from us.

Sounds a bit backward, I know. But according to Scripture, we can live in ways that get God's attention. And as we learn to live each day seeking to connect with God, we are more likely to recognize Him when He responds. Like a child pulling on Dad's pant leg, we have the same power to draw our Father's attention.

Of course, there are challenges—such as the fact that we worship an invisible God.

We can't see God with our eyes or hear Him with our ears, which might explain why we so rarely take a risk to ask Him to show up. Maybe we fear a blocked shot rather than a heart-pounding buzzer shot. We expect God to say "Not today" before He moves on to more important business.

I am familiar with these fears.

But as I began to learn more about what tends to get God's attention, I grew more confident and took bigger risks. The approach will be specific to you and your unique journey with God. But regardless of the path you take, you'll have to take some risks. If connecting with God in special ways were a routine experience, it wouldn't be risky.

Keeping a God-Encounter Secret

There may be much about my encounter that you don't understand. That's what makes such encounters with God *personal*. No one can appreciate them like the person involved, and it's one of the reasons such encounters are best held close.

Many people in the stands enjoyed the buzzer-shot game, and it was fun later, at the end-of-season pizza party, when Gunnar earned the nickname Buzzer Beater on his certificate. But in all the celebration, my silent prayers in the bleachers remained secret. (I did share it with Gunnar after I wrote this book, nearly four years after he tossed up the buzzer shot. And now, you know the story as well.)

I tell the buzzer-shot story because I want Christians to see the treasure of connecting with God. Your Father sees you, He is paying attention, and He wants you to know that.

Yes, faith alone tells me that God fixes His gaze on me. But I know that He is willing to offer more assurance of His presence. Asking God for these moments is not selfish—it is entirely in line with God's desires.

He wants to connect with you in more personal ways. He's interested in every detail of your walk—even when you feel like you've been sent into the desert...with thirsty camels.

6

Meet Steve, Abraham's Chief of Staff

Do you believe God wants to share a buzzer-shot encounter with you? Even if your rational mind struggles with the idea, I suspect your heart is leaning in.

We all go through seasons when we wonder if we even show up on God's home page. Extended periods of silence cause us to be even more convinced that we don't hold God's attention. When we long for memorable moments of connection with God, it is not an indication that we lack faith. It simply means we desire the same thing God desires.

The celebrated heroes of faith in the Bible, from Abraham to Paul, experienced both silence and unique encounters as they walked with God. We see the same reality in the stories of those whose names aren't recorded.

Consider the Story of Steve

Abraham said to his servant, the oldest of his household, who had charge of all that he owned, "… Go to my country and to my relatives, and take a wife for my son Isaac." (Genesis 24:2, 4, NASB)

Abraham probably had dozens of servants, but this guy was the chief. I'm pretty sure his name was Steve. One day Abraham commissioned Steve to undertake an outrageous mission. The servant had to make a journey back to his master's homeland to find a suitable wife for Isaac, Abraham's heir.

Put yourself in Steve's sandals. The lineage of Abraham, God's appointed "father of many nations" (Genesis 17:5), could not be broken. Steve had to find just the right wife for Isaac. He surely knew about the almost-sacrifice of Isaac from years earlier. Who knows, he might even have been part of the famous hill climb. As senior servant or chief of staff, Steve was no stranger to the relationship his master had with God.

Adding to the pressure of this mission, Steve knew that Abraham had full confidence in his abilities. It was expected that the chief servant would return home with just the right wife for Isaac. Steve's task went far beyond simple matchmaking. God's promise to Abraham, and to the world, rested on the successful completion of this assignment.

After a long trek to the old country, Steve entered the city on a Saturday evening (let's pretend). Exhausted from his travels, he spotted what seemed to be the main drag. One hot spot that stood out was a well, a place to get refreshment. Feeling the effects of camel-lag and the weight of the task, Steve called a time-out.

The caravan drew to a halt. Steve wiped his brow and began to survey the scene. Scores of potential brides were carrying vessels to the well.

You can almost hear his thoughts: *O God in heaven, how am I supposed to find a wife for Isaac among total strangers? I could spend days, even months, working my way through the town, interviewing families and surveying prospects. I have to get this right. And it sure would be nice to be finished quickly!*

Sensing an Opportunity

Realizing he was sunk without God's personal touch on this mission, Steve shifted his focus. He began to lay out a sequence of ifs.

O God, *if* You would shine a spotlight on a young lady here, I would approach her and say, "May I have a drink from the well?" And *if* she doesn't slap me for being too forward, and instead says, "Here, have a drink," that would be much appreciated. And *if* she then says, "Let me water your camels too," wow—that would be an exceptional sign.

And Lord, *if* she then follows through on her offer of help, I will know you have given me success. (see Genesis 24:12–14)

Before Steve finished his request to God, his eyes fell on a certain young lady. (He must have prayed with his eyes open.) She was a looker, and more importantly, she was available for marriage. As Steve took off running toward her, he blurted out, "May I have a drink of water from your jar?" And from there, one *if* followed another.

She gave him a drink. Then she offered to water his camels. She poured water from her vessel into a trough and headed back for more. This must have taken awhile because ten camels can drink a lot of water.

Meanwhile, Steve was having a silent, personal encounter with God. "Without saying a word, the man watched her closely to learn whether or not the LORD had made his journey successful" (Genesis 24:21).

Eventually, the camels finished drinking—just as the buzzer sounded. Steve pulled out a velvet box containing a nose ring (how about that, ladies?) and bracelets (see verse 22). Then he did what God's children do when they experience a brain-melting buzzer shot from heaven. He bowed down and worshiped the Lord (see verse 26). God had noticed Steve, heard his request, and delivered a bride for Isaac just like clockwork.

Does this story make Steve seem presumptuous? He sketched out a detailed scenario and asked God to make it happen. But the alternative would have been for the chief of staff to have taken matters into his own hands. He could have canvassed the town, calling on every family that had unmarried daughters. Like so many of us do, Steve could have hunkered down and done this thing through sheer grit and determination.

But Steve had another idea. He asked God to notice him and the situation he was in. He prayed a buzzer-shot prayer, and God wasted no time in answering. God really is available for relationship and help.

Let me say this another way: God is interested in you, and He's waiting for you to engage in a real walk with Him. The basic ingredients of the Christian journey are simple but were never intended to be dull. Maybe that's why Steve's story, and so many others in the Bible, jolt us into looking up and expecting more in our relationship with God.

When it comes to following God, you and I don't want a checklist. We want a living relationship. We were created for a simple, childlike, *different* kind of living.

Not Beginner's Luck

There's a reason we're told that Steve was chief of staff of Abraham's family business. Although Abraham had plenty of relatives who could have been entrusted with the mission of finding a bride for Isaac, Abraham didn't send any of them. Instead, he entrusted Steve—an employee—with the task.

I suspect there were at least two factors at work.

First, Abraham's trust in Steve was built over time. They had walked together for many years, sharing stories of encounters with God. Before receiving the honor of this mission, Steve proved himself in years of wise choices.

Second, Steve's relationship with God was evident. Abraham shared freely with him about God's promises, knowing that his servant was on the same page. Steve's faith, demonstrated in his actions during the search for Isaac's wife, shows an intimacy, trust, and a sense of expectancy with God.

He and Abraham had grown together in faith. This was not Steve's first camel rodeo.

You Too Can Be a Steve

Steve was not the man's real name, of course. But we know he was a man who could be depended on. He was loyal, single-minded, and committed to carrying out his mission. You might identify with Steve in some or all of these ways. He accepted a daunting assignment and succeeded wildly by getting God involved. He took tremendous risks, and God responded. But even with all that, the Bible does not bother to mention his name.

This is another way you might identify with Steve. You might feel like a no-name character. All the more reason to enjoy this demonstration of God's attention, which was focused intently on Steve. You've got a story too. So do I. God is here, and He wants to respond to the steps you take in faith. In that way, you are Steve.

The more I recognize God's interest in me, the more I tend to think and live in ways that show I'm interested in God. Our Father wants both of us to be Steves, looking up to Him in new, secret ways so He can reward us.

Encounters with God might make us feel like children, but these interactions are not all child's play. While it is God's nature to allow us a glimpse of Him when we need it, there's something deeper going on. Often when these God encounters happen, they come at a cost. When you have an unforgettable, buzzer-shot moment, don't be surprised when God calls you to do something unforgettable in return.

Under the Oak Tree

Gideon had a unique encounter with God. An angel showed up under an oak tree while Gideon was working and gave him an assignment from God: he was to deliver the Israelites from the Midianites! But Gideon wanted to know for sure that he was actually hearing from God, so he asked boldly, "Give me a sign that it is really you talking to me" (Judges 6:17).

Have you ever felt like that, wanting proof that it really is God's voice that you are hearing?

God gave Gideon a sign using a neat little fireworks display, a chunk of meat, and some bread on an altar. Gideon was overwhelmed. But then again, God had asked him to do something that would take a surpassing amount of courage. In light of the task, Gideon wanted a bit more of a connection and further proof of God's presence. So he asked for another sign, and this time he laid out some ifs.

Putting out a fleece, he told God: "If there is dew on the fleece but the ground is dry in the morning, I'll take that as an awesome sign." Guess what? Gideon got the buzzer shot. It happened just as he prescribed.

Still desiring more, a *third* sign, Gideon next specified the opposite condition: "If the fleece is dry and the ground is wet tomorrow morning, that will boost my faith even more." So God gave him yet another buzzer shot. Three in a row!

What Gideon didn't know is that for each buzzer shot God gave him, God was going to stretch his faith accordingly. With each buzzer shot, Gideon's army was shrinking in size—from thirty-two thousand to ten thousand to three hundred soldiers.

Gideon learned that an encounter with God comes at a cost. It required him to change the way he approached the battle against the Midianites. He did not have the benefit of being able to read the story in advance. He was taking a risk, and he later was required to take additional steps of faith.

God came through, and the battle was won by a ridiculously small army. We can imagine Gideon calling a time-out after the battle was won, looking up with a smile or maybe falling to his knees. Not only had he won a victory, he had also felt God's watchfulness along the way.

You Are Significant Too

Gideon wanted God's attention, and he got it three times. Then he led a stunning military victory. Abraham's chief of staff, Steve, took off for a faraway land, arrived in a foreign city without even knowing the local protocol, and sought God's attention in the form of help in finding a bride for Isaac.

I was in a gym watching my son play basketball. I was talking to God in my heart while watching the game, and I felt God's gaze in a buzzer shot. I admit my basketball moment was not on a par with Gideon's or Steve's. My son's shot going in at the last second might not shape Kingdom history.

But for what I was seeking—a connection with God that could not be overlooked—being noticed by Him ranked right up there with Steve at the well searching for Isaac's match. Even with all the important things going on in the world, my world—and what was happening in it—was of concern to God. In that moment, I knew without question that *God sees me.*

And you know what? God sees you too. But you need your own moment. God desires to have these encounters *for* you and *with* you.

We live in a broken world, and many of us struggle with our broken lives. God is concerned about the tragedy and suffering of humanity, and He is also interested in you personally. You might have a loving family, a comfortable place to live, and food in the fridge. Or you might have lost those things and the people closest to you. Either way, God's attention is not limited. He sees you, and He wants you to see and hear Him as well.

Buzzer-shot encounters with God come in many forms. For you, it could come on the heels of a prayer of ifs. But it might be in response to something very different. We are only starting to explore the many ways we can connect with God.

Growing While Walking

When you have a buzzer-shot encounter with God, your hope is restored. God lets you know you have His attention, then He asks you to take a risk of faith. He raises the bar.

Gideon got God's attention more than once. Then he had to go into battle with a downsized army. David watched sheep and received God's help when he protected them from lions and bears. Then the young shepherd faced down a giant. We don't know the rest of Steve's story, but I suspect God raised the bar for his faith also. As chief of staff for the father of many nations, who knows what he might have been asked to do.

And me? I prayed for a simple thing. God heard me, let me know He noticed, and then called me to greater accountability. I want you to realize that much more is available to you in your walk with God. Are you waiting on a sign? You have God's attention. His loving face is on you. Your Father is waiting for a sign from *you*.

7

God Is a Smitten Father

The day our first child was born began with Stephanie and me playing cards on the living-room floor. It was just past midnight and she knew something was about to happen. Her suitcase and makeup bag were packed and ready, left just inside the front door. She kept a log and a stopwatch by her side as our card game continued into the early morning hours.

During contractions, she did rhythmic-breathing drills and monitored the clock while I enjoyed snacks and managed the TV remote. At some point I went to bed. She never did. When I woke up around six that morning, I found she was still in the living room with her stopwatch and notebook.

We had the day off from work so we kept playing cards. Finally, in the afternoon, it was time to go.

I sweated bullets on the drive across town as I noticed the fuel-gauge needle was dancing in the red zone. I have a bad habit of playing chicken with the gas tank. It adds a little adventure to any car trip when you match your wits against a fuel gauge and continually recalculate how many miles you can cover before the tank runs dry.

This time the game wasn't fun. I was scared.

We made it to the hospital parking lot. I grabbed Stephanie's bags and helped her out of the car. As she stopped to take a rest at the curb, a lady came out of the ER pushing a wheelchair. With my wife safely in the chair, I breathed a sigh of relief.

The rest of the day passed fairly quickly—for me anyway. Stephanie put on a hospital gown, sat on a bed, and then she gave birth. (She tells a longer, more animated, version of the day's events.) A nurse handed me some giant scissors. I cut the cord. And what happened next slowed things down.

A Father's Face

A baby boy was placed in my arms, and I melted like warm butter. Whatever problems were in my life at that moment vanished as I stared into my child's face.

I wasn't sure if I should touch him; I had never done this before. The nods in the room served as my permission. Slowly I touched his little nose, his checks, his chin, his ears. The whole world stopped as I stood gazing at my son.

There was no whooping and hollering on my part—no hugging the nurse or passing around cigars. I just stood there gazing, marveling at my son. If it was possible for my face to glow, it did at that moment. My eyes were fixed on a tiny infant who bore my name and resembled so much about me.

Ten years had passed since I caught my dad watching me on the golf course, just before I teed off at a junior tournament. Even though he was standing at a distance and I couldn't quite make out his face, I knew he was watching me. And I had a pretty good idea what he was thinking. I was never far from my dad's thoughts, and often I was not outside his gaze.

After a decade more of life and experience, as I stood in the delivery room and cradled my newborn son, I had a similar moment of my own. This time I was the father, gazing at my son.

I was so pleased.

God Enamored

It's not hard for me to imagine God being enamored of His children. The young sons of Adam and Eve were surely adorable in His sight. I wonder if God held Cain and Abel, earth's first infants, with obvious delight. I wonder if He played with them when they were young boys. How quickly did separation set in, first between God and the people He created, and then between God and the children of Adam and Eve? How quickly did God become invisible to them?

However it transpired, God still found pleasing moments to enjoy with His children. The world changes, but God's heart is constant. No matter what we might do, our Father's eyes are fixed on us.

We know that Cain killed Abel. The first murder is stark evidence of how Cain lost sight of God's face.

But in the midst of violence and upheaval, we have the surprising account of Abel's gift. He presented a lamb to God as an offering. Something about this rocked God's heart—in a pleasing way.

The Bible uses the Hebrew word *sha'ah* to describe God's reaction to Abel's actions (see Genesis 4:4). In the Hebrew, God was "gazing, fixing eyes, looking intently" upon Abel and his gift. Abel received a personal reaction from God!

This must have sent Abel's heart into orbit, but Cain had a very different reaction. Because of Abel's gift and God's pleasure, Abel is mentioned first among the faith heroes who left a God-pleasing legacy (see Hebrews 11:1–4). God looked intently on the brother who brought a pleasing gift, which should encourage us as we seek to walk with God, knowing He sees us.

Often it's Cain's distinction as earth's first murderer that stands out in our minds with this account. But from God's perspective, it is the pleasing memory of Abel that survives into the New Testament, and today.

When Austin was a toddler, Stephanie and I would drop him off in the nursery at church. As new parents do, in between services we'd go back for a peek through the one-way window into the room where he played. While we watched him he might look our way, but since he couldn't see us through the mirror, he'd go on playing, oblivious to our watching.

Occasionally our little boy would see something move behind the glass, enough for him to stare a little longer. He might even make out his mother's silhouette, just enough to know it was her. Even with this faint glimpse, he'd break into a giant smile and start bouncing on the rocking horse, cooing and slobbering and living it up. He was basking in our watchfulness. Meanwhile we basked in his awareness of our watching him.

I believe something like this was happening between God and Abel.

God Likes to Be Pleased

God has a history of marveling at His children. And history is filled with children seeking to please God—many of whom are mentioned in Hebrews 11. Immediately following the mention of Abel and his pleasing legacy, we learn about Enoch. He is "one who *pleased God*" (verse 5). I want that in my bio: *one who pleased God!*

The Bible says Enoch "walked with God" (Genesis 5:22, 24). One day he was walking around town. The next day he was reported as a missing person. He had been taken up to heaven.

The next character mentioned in Hebrews is Noah (see 11:7). He "found favor in the eyes of the LORD" and "walked with God" (Genesis 6:8–9).

Even Jesus sought to please His Heavenly Father. Jesus said, "for I always do what *pleases* him" (John 8:29). This makes sense. In the New Testament, the two occasions God's voice is heard booming from the heavens, we hear these words: "This is my Son, whom I love; with him I am well *pleased*" (Matthew 3:17; 17:5).

Even for children, the basic message of pleasing God is clearly stated: "Children, obey your parents in everything, for this *pleases* the Lord" (Colossians 3:20). Paul affirmed the importance of pleasing God, noting it always will be our goal to *please* Him whether we are on earth or in heaven (see 2 Corinthians 5:9).

Pleasing our Father is central to His heart and to our walk.

Acceptable to God

There's another word in the Bible most people don't grasp, and that's unfortunate because this word will change the way we look at so many key scriptures. It's the word *acceptable*. It means "pleasing."

Check out Psalm 19 where David wrote, "Let the words of my mouth and the meditation of my heart be *acceptable* in your sight" (verse 14, ESV). Depending on your Bible version, the word might be *pleasing* instead of *acceptable*.

Paul's teaching was consistent with David's prayer. Paul told Christians to "present your bodies as a living sacrifice, holy and acceptable to God" (Romans 12:1, ESV). Pleasing God, then enjoying a fatherly reaction from Him, has been the pattern since Adam. So why are many of us uncomfortable with this concept?

Bad Dads and Bad Doctrine

The idea of pleasing God is under attack. It doesn't sit well for some, and it can actually be a turnoff, like an unexpected wave of onion breath.

For some, the doctrine of pleasing God has been likened to appeasing, or working to satisfy, an overbearing God who can never be satisfied, much less delighted with us. Where does this tainted view come from?

Much of it stems from heavily dysfunctional father-child relationships. Many men and women have been hurt by negative experiences with earthly fathers (and mothers too). The children, now grown and many with children of their own, will never forget the pain and difficulty of trying to measure up to the demands of a mother or a father who, no matter what, could never be pleased.

The demanding, even abusive, treatment received from parents shapes what many of us expect from God. We assume we'll never be able to please Him. As a result, we journey through life with a broken view of God. In our thinking, God can't possibly be happy with us. But we couldn't be more wrong.

Our View Shapes Our Actions

In Jesus's famous parable of the talents (see Matthew 25:14–30), three servants each received a specific sum of money and were told to grow its value. Two of them invested the sum and showed a handsome return. The third servant sat on his principal and did nothing.

He blamed his lousy performance on an overbearing master, one he believed could never be pleased. Since he was convinced his master would never be satisfied, he decided there was no reward for taking a risk. His view was faulty, and he was held accountable. His master rebuked him for his laziness. The tragedy is that this outcome easily could have been avoided by having a proper view of God.

Many Christians live with a false view of the Master. They don't believe God can be pleased and therefore have no motivation to try living differently. Why would they take risks to walk more closely with God when they already are convinced that their Father has lost patience with them?

After reading my book *Plastic Donuts,* a woman contacted me to share her story of sexual abuse. Her father, a man known as a spiritual leader, had abused her when she was young. Later she received decades of counseling to work through the pain, guilt, and shame resulting from her lost innocence.

Reading about God's fatherly love, she saw for the first time that God seeks a close relationship with her. Her concept of God changed when she could understand Him as a perfect, loving Father.

Don't let bad dads (or even good dads with imperfections) cause you to accept bad doctrine. We were created to please God. If you try on this perspective in light of Scripture, you'll be surprised just how good, right, and true it is. More importantly, you'll see how much you really need it.

Deep down, we all desire to please others, and we desire to be pleased by others. Even Maslow's hierarchy of needs recognizes that beyond our basic need for air, food, water, safety, and protection, people need love, affection, and esteem.

The need for mutually pleasing relationships was orchestrated by God. That is why He created Eve for Adam, and Adam for Eve. And that is why God created Adam and Eve (and you and me) for Himself. God takes pleasure in His children.

Pleasing Purpose

Our purpose in life is to please God. From the beginning, God wanted us to be present with Him and to share His delight. This means our original purpose was not to evangelize the world. This came later, after the first couple's dreadful fruit salad. But before there was distance between God and humanity, there was the desire God had for us.

As pleasing God remains at the core of our being, it's also at the core of our faith expression. When we live by faith, we please God. Hebrews 11:6 says, "And without faith it is impossible to *please* God…"

But the sentence doesn't end there, and the second part of the verse is crucial and tells us what faith really is: "…because anyone who comes to him must believe that he exists and that he rewards those who *earnestly seek* him" (Hebrews 11:6). The writer of Hebrews links our childlike belief in rewards from God to faith that pleases God.

When you believe in God's existence *and* you seek after Him, expecting a reward, then your faith is at work and God is pleased. You're not being selfish or self-centered or narcissistic. You are simply taking God's Word at face value. You are following the guidance of Jesus and Paul, as well as the examples of a roll call of biblical heroes and heroines. From God's perspective, good things flow when His children take noticeable steps to seek Him. God rewards that type of living.

Often we teach children (and adults) the first part of the faith equation (believing in God) but not the second part (seeking God). The faith heroes mentioned in Hebrews 11 were commended not just for believing, but also for seeking God's reward.

We'll talk more about rewards in a later chapter. For now, we'll simply acknowledge that they include heavenly rewards as well as the earthly kind. And yes, this includes encounters with God such as buzzer shots.

God uses a wide assortment of rewarding mechanisms to say, "I see you, and I'm pleased!"

Seeking is about pleasing God, and pleasing God brings joy and delight to Him. You and I were created for this.

Pleasing God and Doing Stuff

Christians often get nervous when we talk about seeking to please God. *Seeking* sounds a lot like working, striving, taking initiative, and hoping to achieve a result. Those who resist such notions emphasize being instead of doing. Just be with God. Be content in God alone. Don't get worked up about doing religious stuff.

Perhaps you've heard these ideas?

Sure, there are times when doing gets in the way of being. But as we are seeing from Scripture, being *involves* doing. The two are not easily separated. While I can be with my wife and enjoy her presence, at some point I need to be active in the relationship.

Being in relationship involves participation. Being in a *great* relationship involves extra mindfulness and intentional actions so two people can stay connected. And because I love my wife and want to please her, doing things becomes a natural outflow of my being a husband to her. The same goes for our relationship with God.

These essentials—believing in God's presence and seeking Him, while believing that He rewards those who please Him—are critical as we talk more about doing. If you hold to the mistaken idea that pleasing God means performing or appeasing or working under pressure, then your walk with God will bring little joy.

But if you expect good things from God, and know He's deeply interested in you, walking with Him will open up your heart. You will embrace new activities. Your walk with God will feel like a relationship, not a religion. It will bring you joy, not more obligations. When pleasing God makes sense to you, you'll aim to bring Him delight, and you will know He's pleased with you.

When you embrace this idea of pleasing God, you'll be that much closer to experiencing the ultimate rewards that come from walking with God: feeling His pleasure, sensing His smile, hearing divine applause.

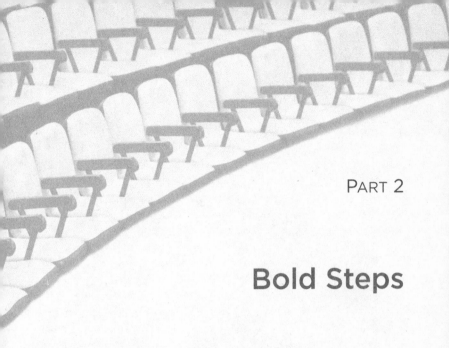

PART 2

Bold Steps

Seeing God differently is a start to your fresh walk with God. But it's the *living differently* that's crucial. Too many people are struggling in their faith, not believing they can have a close walk with God. But instead of giving up, turning off your heart, and intellectualizing God, it's time to do something. Take some actual steps.

For starters, Jesus gave us the secret ingredients in Matthew 6! While these are things every Christian has heard about, read about, and maybe even practiced, we're going to look at them in a different light. These secret steps are not items on a task list. They are ways of connecting with God and putting ourselves in position to notice Him noticing us.

As we look at these steps, I'll unpack some personal stories. Yes, some more buzzer-shot encounters and surprises.

While I'm not always as mindful of God's presence as I'd like, the good news is that God is extremely patient. He does not penalize us for missed opportunities. Whatever connections we think we've missed along the way, a fresh opportunity always awaits us. And the step that's directly in front of us is the one that matters. Let's begin.

8

The Unexpected Visitor

After working five years as an accountant followed by five years as a stock trader, my career clock suggested I was due for something new. God's bridge for me was a consulting gig.

In some cases, consulting is a job you get when a company is willing to pay you to tell them what they can easily find out from their own employees—but they'd rather have you do it. Consultants find these jobs when they're either really good at what they do and can charge lots of money, or when they are confused about their lives and not sure what to do next. I was the second kind.

It was Friday afternoon, and I was two days away from leaving on a three-week overseas business trip. My mind was cluttered with details and tasks I needed to complete before leaving the country.

I'd been overseas before, but this trip would be different. My itinerary had me traveling through several European countries to manage a string of sticky business meetings. Every company on the list would be dreading my arrival (does the word *audit* sound appealing to you?). Not exactly Travel Channel material.

With two months' planning behind me, I had lined up rental cars and hotel rooms, confirmed meeting schedules, and finalized my daily agendas. While my departure was still forty-eight hours away, my mind was already somewhere over the Atlantic.

Still, I knew I needed to accomplish a few simpler things before I left.

The next item on my punch list was a haircut. Austin, then a six-year-old, was with me as we ran errands. It was a chance to pal around together before my trip.

Arriving on a Winter Breeze

It was an unusually cold winter day, with dreary gray skies and leftover snow on the ground. Austin and I entered the little white house that now housed a hair salon.

It was the kind of place where you sit on velvet furniture in the lobby, surrounded by green-faced women who have tin foil sparkling in their hair. The salon sold thirty-dollar bottles of shampoo and offered an array of cosmetic services from facials to foot rubs. My friend Rick owned the salon, which was my excuse for choosing such a beauty-oriented establishment.

Austin and I were sitting in the lobby trying to exude masculinity when the front door cracked open. The first thing that came through was a forty-mile-per-hour blast of frozen air. That got everyone's attention, and we were curious about what might come through next. It appeared to be…the front end of a shopping cart, like the nose of a Kroger icebreaker.

Eventually, a gray-haired head peeked in. An elderly lady was trying to push the shopping cart through the doorway. She stared at us and mumbled something.

Awkwardness overpowered the scent of nail-polish remover. Like synchronized swimmers, we turned toward the receptionist as if to say, *Do something. You're in charge.* Her front-desk training likely covered solicitors, but this visitor was different. Not having any idea what the lady had said, the receptionist broke the ice with "You'll need to talk to the manager."

I knew Rick was probably up to his elbows in burnt-red hair dye. I also knew the receptionist had issued the generic nonresponse in hopes that the visitor would go away. I could sense that everyone was thinking, *Someone get her out of here, then shut the door.* Or maybe that's what was in *my* head. But I couldn't stand to see the elderly lady waiting, yet not getting a reaction from anyone.

So I walked to the door to help her...back outside. Once we were outdoors, I asked, "What is it that you need?"

"Rice and beans," she responded in a quivering voice. "I'm looking for rice and beans."

I heard what she said, but it didn't register. She must have sensed my confusion because before I could respond, she said, "Food. Does anyone have any food?"

Frozen by a Question

We all know what it's like to be approached for money while walking down a street, stopped at a traffic light, or gassing up our car. But this situation was different.

Maybe the woman thought the salon was a house? Seeing that the lights were on, she might have expected to find a warm kitchen. Maybe a hot meal.

Whatever her situation, it was obvious she had a great need. Still, I had a to-do list on my mind, and the clock was ticking before I boarded a flight for London. But the woman's need grabbed my attention. I knew she had God's attention too.

I reached in my pocket and pulled out a twenty-dollar bill. I gave it to her and asked, "What will you do?" She said something about a grocery store several blocks away. I nodded, getting the idea while also wanting to get back inside. She positioned the shopping cart back onto the walkway and headed toward the street as I ducked back into the little white house.

When my turn came for a haircut, I didn't tell Rick about the surprise visitor. Instead, we chatted about normal stuff—our families, our businesses, the weather, and the weekend at hand. Meanwhile, overseas travel weighed heavily on my mind.

Afterward, Austin and I got in the car to head home. As we approached the nearby supermarket, I decided to pull into the parking lot to see if the gray-haired lady was around. Part of me hoped we wouldn't find her, but there was another part of me that did.

At the store entrance a warm blast of air knocked the remaining clippings from my head. We walked toward a random aisle, and there she was. Even though I was looking for her, I was still surprised to see her again. She was reaching for something high on a shelf. As I glanced down at her other hand, I noticed the twenty-dollar bill clutched in her fist.

In front of her was a shopping cart. *Surely that's not the same cart she used to ram the salon door,* I wondered. The cart was empty except for a small bag resting at the bottom. It was a bag of beans.

The image is etched in my mind: a large shopping cart carrying only one small bag of beans.

I looked up to see what she was retrieving from the shelf. My heart melted…

It was a bag of rice.

In My Court

There was no turning back now. I introduced myself…again (more formally this time). I learned her name was Mrs. Whyte. I introduced her to Austin, then offered to push the cart for her. Mrs. Whyte was walking to my right while Austin was on my left. The three of us stretched across the aisle.

I clumsily hinted that I'd be picking up the tab. She seemed to understand, so around the store we went. I began to pray silently, desperately. I knew God's eyes were shining a spotlight on the scene. The Bible says so much about the poor—the "least of these," as Jesus calls them. This shopping trip was outside my comfort zone and definitely outside my task list, but I had embraced the divine appointment God inserted into my day.

I sputtered the next question that came to mind. "Do you know Jesus?"

That seemed to shift the conversation to another level. "Ohhh yes! I know my sweet Jesus," she said. Seeing the intensity in her brown eyes, I knew she meant those words.

Sensing that the everyday stuff of life was a challenge for her, I offered some words of encouragement about her future home in heaven. She seemed to embrace the ideas more deeply than I did, which really got me thinking. I wondered if it was because she experienced less comfort and warmth on earth than most people in this country do.

As I probed into Mrs. Whyte's life circumstances, I learned she was in a housing transition. She had a new apartment, but was without food. Things were starting to make a bit more sense. Still, my mind flooded with questions.

As we walked the aisles and filled up the cart, I began sending buzzer-shot requests to God. *Lord, give me the words for Mrs. Whyte. What do You want me to say? What does she need?*

I was happy to buy her some groceries. Still, I sensed there must be something more to this encounter. I paid for the items, then we walked toward the bus stop at the edge of the parking lot.

What happened next took this encounter to a whole new level. It was a conversation I will never forget.

I said, "Mrs. Whyte, if you will share some of your food with some-one in need, Jesus will see it, He will be pleased, and He will reward you one day in heaven."

Then I looked at the twenty-dollar bill still clutched in her fist. "If you will share some of this money also, Jesus will see it, He will be pleased, and He will reward you for that too."

She thanked me just as the bus shushed to a stop.

Austin and I helped her step up into the bus with several bags of groceries. As my son and I drove off toward home, that's when I heard the voice.

A-i-r b-a-l-l! You totally missed it.

Did I really say those things? "Give away some of your rice and beans, and some of your twenty dollars. Jesus will see it, and He will re-ward you." Was this really the right message for a lady like Mrs. Whyte? Maybe I hadn't heard God.

One time God used a donkey to speak, so I figured He could use me. But my words felt so empty and misguided.

On the other hand, I really believed what I said. That's the message in the Secret Sermon, right? Jesus would see her gifts, and He would be pleased. Of all the ways I could have helped Mrs. Whyte in that moment, sharing those words felt right.

I went back and forth on this, and that's how it is sometimes when you walk in relationship with an invisible God. It's not like sitting down for coffee with a friend, hearing the vocal inflections and reading body language. Sometimes, with God, you're just not sure.

An Unexpected Replay with Mrs. Whyte

As often is true of the Christian journey, time changes everything. Time gave new meaning to the words that I had spoken to Mrs. Whyte.

In the grocery store, I had asked God what she needed. Instead, He gave me the words that *I* needed. It would take some time for me to fully grasp how significant those instructions were. What felt like an air ball was actually a game changer. A slow-motion buzzer shot.

God watches us more closely than we think. When we take a shot, we trust that He sees it and guides it, even if it bounces around awhile.

9

Giving Away Your
Rice and Beans

After spending nearly two decades on the mission field, Jason and Sarah returned to the United States with their eight children. A sticky political situation had developed abroad, forcing them to flee for their safety.

Each family member went through US customs with only a single backpack containing their possessions. The youngest child was in diapers. The oldest was a teenager.

They settled near Sarah's parents. Several families stepped in to help meet their basic needs. A rental house was provided, furniture appeared, kitchen cabinets were filled with food, and some cash gifts showed up.

Stephanie and I became point persons for collecting some of the gifts, giving us a chance to bond with Jason and Sarah. I liked being around Jason and was drawn to his rugged approach to faith. Something about his walk seemed risky—in a good way.

In due time, he found a job. But with a family of ten and still adjusting to the cost of living, he needed outside help to get the financial engine cranking. Cash gifts were still coming in, but this was a revenue stream that would end. I offered to help Jason get a handle on his finances. This would involve some budget coaching—you know, working on spreadsheets and maybe implementing a cash-in-envelopes system to channel spending. He was grateful for the offer and eager to learn.

The Budget Guy

On a Friday afternoon, Jason and I met at a sandwich shop. I had brought along a one-thousand dollar gift from various contributors. We discussed a strategy for how best to make use of these precious funds. Several days later, we met again. Jason mentioned that the money was gone. I tried not to appear surprised, but I let him know I was curious.

Jason and Sarah had given the cash gift to another missionary family that had passed through the area. "They needed the money more than we did," he said. He described all this as if we were discussing the weather. As if having to provide for a family of ten and giving away one thousand dollars was a completely normal thing to do.

I took a deep breath and leaned back in my chair. *Did he really just give away the gift? I wonder what the contributors will think about that! Shouldn't he have used the money for food, diapers, or a rainy-day fund?*

I was supposed to be the budget guy, the financial geek who would help this precious family get back on their feet after having to leave their adopted country. I had brought my carefully prepared folders to continue our talk of gradually building back financial stability for Jason's family. But after he told me about the thousand dollars, I slid my folder filled with forms back into my bag. I looked at my new friend and thought, *We can have this budget conversation later, or maybe never!*

And that is when I thought back to another friend I'd met a year earlier, Mrs. Whyte. I had paid for her groceries, walked her to a bus stop, and instructed her to share what little she had. In her case, it was a twenty-dollar bill and some rice and beans. I had encouraged her to give from her very limited possessions.

That's essentially what Jason and Sarah had done. They gave to another family from their very limited provisions. They gave the "rice and beans" from their family's cupboard.

Prophet Talk

It's surprising how frequently the New Testament mentions money and giving. It's a core theme in Matthew 6, in the Secret Sermon where Jesus talked about doing things secretly and receiving a reward from God. But even before Jesus took on the subject of giving, John the Baptist already had started the ball rolling.

John was an extreme risk taker. His advice to King Herod cost him his head, which was delivered to the king on a platter.

One day John was preaching (okay, more like yelling) a serious, in-your-face message. He wanted the crowd to know that coming to the river for a dunk-shot baptism would not be enough to save their souls. His message introduced the idea of bearing the fruit of repentance (see Luke 3:8–9). The crowd seemed interested, so they asked, "To bear this kind of repenting fruit, what should we do?"

Unlike some consultants who use lots of words to say very little, John used a few words to say a lot. "Anyone who has two shirts should share with the one who has none, and anyone who has food should do the same" (Luke 3:11, NIV 2011).

Be a giver. Sounds pretty basic, doesn't it? In the economy of repentance and bearing fruit—which is the life John was talking about—spreadsheets and the bottom line don't always apply. He was talking about risky faith.

His advice was aimed at everyone in the crowd, which we can assume included everyone from the well-heeled folks to the down-and-out folks. This giving way of life was for everyone.

Maybe that's why Jesus says in His Secret Sermon, "*when* you give," not *if* you give (Matthew 6:2).

Stewardship Lessons

In the past I was a volunteer financial counselor for my church. I helped people create and stick to a budget, spend less money than they earned, and focus on getting out of debt. All these practices constitute what we Christians often refer to as "good stewardship."

But my encounters with Mrs. Whyte and Jason messed with my stewardship mind-set.

As I walked the aisles of a supermarket with Mrs. Whyte, collecting basic provisions for her next meal, I was not thinking about her need for a budget or a cash-envelope system. Instead, I was thinking about her opportunity to share from her possessions, something she was able to do immediately.

When I sat with Jason and listened to him share how he gave away one thousand dollars, I was reminded of the same basic truth: giving is not what you do after you straighten out your finances. Giving is what you do when you straighten out your heart.

I've been part of plenty of stewardship conversations and know what you might be thinking. You might wonder if my friend Jason was neglecting his responsibilities to his uprooted family. Or perhaps you are curious about their bigger financial picture. Did Jason and Sarah have debt? (They didn't.) Were they living off government support? (Nope.)

You might be imagining a church benevolence-fund disbursement manual. If a family is in need and they are given one thousand dollars, and they promptly give the gift to someone else, are they entitled to further assistance?

How can we try to make sense of Jason's decision making?

What I learned from Jason was this: when it gets down to the basics of living, you give. Even if you are living in a borrowed apartment, your family's personal belongings fit into several backpacks, and your income doesn't come close to supporting a family of ten. Still, you can give.

And if you're like Mrs. Whyte, down to a few bags of groceries and a twenty-dollar bill, you can give from that too.

Giving is for everyone.

Gifts That Impact God?

Serious talk about giving makes people break out in hives. When John was preaching to the crowd about giving, I'm sure his words made them squirm. Squirming is expected, but that is no reason to avoid the subject. In order to get a clear look at giving, it helps to understand the three parties to our gifts.

First, there's the recipient. Our gifts can fund the work of the church, heal the sick, spread the gospel, feed the hungry, care for orphans.

Giving is good for the giver too. Jesus said when we give in secret, our Father will reward us. And these rewards take on a variety of forms. There is a third party to our giving. It is God. We give because we are children seeking to please our Father. Our gifts impact Him personally. Remember Abel's gift that attracted God's gaze? The memory of that gift remained etched in God's heart. That's why even today God boasts about the gift (see Hebrews 11:4). Think of this like a child's drawing that still is displayed on God's fridge so all the family (that's us) can see it.

Even before humankind was needy—back when there were no orphans, no homelessness, no hunger or thirst—gifts were given to God. This was true long before His children were in need of charity from each other. In other words, giving was not directed toward God so that it could be used for ministry and humanitarian purposes. The gifts were *for* God, although He was in need of nothing.

Still, God always has desired a connection with us. And in the same way that gifts connect us to one another, giving connects us to our Father in heaven.

Paul wanted the first-century Christians to know their cash gifts to him were a "fragrant offering, an *acceptable* sacrifice, pleasing to God" (Philippians 4:18). Their gifts not only met Paul's personal needs, but also brought pleasure to God.

We're bombarded by fund-raising appeals. Many of the needs are legitimate and important, but right now we are not talking about meeting the needs of the world. Instead, we're talking about our need to connect with God and His desire for us to be connected to Him. As we talk about giving, we must step back to see the big picture.

According to statistics, Christian giving is generally pretty pathetic. Many Christians and churches consider 10 percent as a minimum standard (an idea we'll look at later). But recent studies show that churchgoing Christians in the United States give an average of 2 to 3 percent of their incomes to churches and nonprofits.

While these trends are disturbing to churches and ministries trying to fund operating budgets, it also speaks to something much more serious. Giving is our way of telling God how much we value our walk with Him.

When Gifts and Budgets Collide

Why are we talking about giving? Because it's one of the secret ingredients Jesus mentioned in His Secret Sermon. It's one of the ways we step into our relationship with God. And in response to our gifts, God likes to show us that He notices. Often He lets us know of His delight through a gift of His own. Jesus calls these "rewards." You could call them blessings or even kickbacks. I know the term may strike you as odd in this context, but let's take a closer look.

Connected to the Secret Sermon in Matthew 6, Jesus tells us to give freely (storing up treasure in heaven) and to not worry about our basic needs—food, clothing, shelter. Why? He said our Father would provide these things (see verses 25–34). God sees us and our sacrifices. He has our back.

"Look at the birds of the air," Jesus said. "They do not sow or reap or store away in barns, and yet your heavenly Father feeds them. Are you not much more valuable than they?" (Matthew 6:26).

Jesus likened us to birds and grass. Those are living things that don't worry about clothing, housing, or their next meal. So why should we worry? (That's not just me asking, by the way.)

If Jason and Sarah choose to give away one thousand dollars that would have gone far in supplying their family with basic provisions, God has their backs. He'll provide what they need. If Mrs. Whyte gives from her meager possessions, including from her food and her small amount of cash, God has her back. (He was taking care of her even when He directed her to the little white house in search of a rice-and-beans meal.)

God sees and promises to meet our basic needs, even when we give outside the budget and don't follow the accepted rules of sound financial management. He is pleased with our gifts even when they seem irresponsible by the world's standards; even when we fail to follow the guidelines for sound stewardship.

Sounds crazy, doesn't it?

But let's face it: most of us are not living like birds and grass. Who never worries about getting the bills paid, making the rent, and wondering how we'll make do with the rising cost of gas and groceries? And what about those of us who like to have a few extra shirts in the closet, you know, savings for retirement or college or that rainy-day situation?

Does God's constant awareness of our lives and interest in our giving extend to those of us who have three, six, or even twelve months' cash sitting in a bank account?

The Controversy Surrounding Rewards

Picture a single mom who begins to tithe for the first time. Shortly afterward she receives an unexpected raise at work. Or a couple commits to give a faith-testing gift from their savings, then they receive an unexpected tax refund of a similar amount. Or a family gives away a car, then someone gives them a nicer car than the one they gave away.

We've all heard stories such as these. Perhaps you've had a similar experience in your giving journey. The reason this happens is because God gets our attention when our gifts get His attention.

Still, people often get testy when Christians suggest that God blesses those who give. The extreme version of such blessing talk is known as prosperity theology, the idea that God will prosper your wealth and health in direct response to your faith and good deeds. This theology is toxic, even wicked at times. It motivates people to do the right thing for the wrong reasons.

But one thing about bad doctrines is they're often born from deep-rooted biblical truth. That's the case with prosperity teaching. Dozens of scriptures mention the blessings (rewards) and favor of God that rest on those who give and share generously with the poor. Just read Proverbs.

Still, it's not a clear-cut doctrine. At least not in the way we experience it.

Job's friends subscribed to the prosperity principle; in fact, their counsel to Job was based on a view that bad things must have happened to him because of his behavior. In other words, God was punishing him because he deserved it. (God chastised the friends later for their misguided advice.)

Solomon, the wisest man ever, saw problems with prosperity thinking; he found it perplexing that often the righteous get what the wicked deserve (suffering) while the wicked get what the righteous deserve (prosperity) (see Ecclesiastes 8:14).

So what are we to make of all this? Does God reward givers in material ways?

Paul wrote, "whoever sows generously will also reap generously" (2 Corinthians 9:6). Personally, I've experienced some buzzer-shot rewards after giving. I have talked with countless givers, and they all acknowledge that God's faithfulness and provision are clear in their lives.

These rewards often are received when God's children step out in unusual ways—in ways we might think of as risky faith. When you explore new frontiers—such as giving for the first time, increasing your giving percentage, giving away a tax refund or year-end bonus, giving from the down payment you saved for a home—God notices because He understands what this gift means to you. Even if your giving is from an abundance of possessions, and not from the last of your rice and beans, it's God's nature to respond.

When you step out and take risks, seeking a connection with God, rewards happen. But to understand this truth biblically, we need to understand what is going on behind God's rewards.

Don't Miss What Is Happening

Remember, when you experience buzzer-shot blessings from heaven, God is connecting with you. These rewards are personal encounters with the living God that should get your attention and warrant your worship, love, and praise.

When Peter was fishing and heard Jesus call out to him to throw the nets to the other side of the boat, his obedience resulted in an overflowing haul of fish. Peter was awestruck by the catch. But he seemed to be even more overwhelmed by the encounter with Jesus. There was no denying that Jesus had noticed him. So Peter got out of the boat and took off toward Jesus, leaving the fish behind (see John 21:7).

Receiving a reward from God is wonderful, whether a surprise bonus at work; an unexpected gift from a friend, a relative, or even a stranger; or some other financial reward. But don't forget what's really happening. God is connecting with you. When God kicks back financial rewards to you, He is saying, *I see you. I noticed that. I'm watching you. You are pleasing to Me!* God wants you to recognize that He recognizes you and wants to get personally involved in your circumstances.

When Gunnar's last-second shot dropped into the basket, I could have jumped out of the bleachers and run to the floor to celebrate with others. But if I had joined in, I would have cut short my moment of God connecting with me. So instead my response was to pause, look up, and worship my Father.

When you experience God's financial rewards in response to your giving, it should bring you to your knees. Think about what is happening from God's macro view. While givers and receivers all around the world are sending love and praise to God, He is showering us with gifts (rewards) from heaven. This is how God's giving economy works.

Taking Risks with Your Giving

An acquaintance of mine attended a church that issued a tithing challenge. The challenge was this: if you commit to giving 10 percent of your income to the church and, afterward, you do not experience blessings from God, the church will refund your money.

After a season of tithing, this man did not notice the level of changes he expected, so he quit giving. In his mind, the guarantee had not worked.

Instead of looking to God for a personal connection, he was looking to a church for a particular outcome. And when he didn't get the experience he expected, he gave in to disappointment.

God is not a slot machine that owes us a payoff for putting in a quarter. God's tangible blessings are not cosmic laws of the universe that are triggered every time we give.

Rather, God's response to our giving is similar to His responses to our prayers. I don't always get an immediate answer; sometimes I get silence. I don't always experience physical healing; I still wear hearing aids. In the same way, giving is a faith journey. And often, our faith is tested.

Some people like to quote Malachi 3:10, where God said, "Test me in this…and see if I will not throw open the floodgates of heaven." But we need to keep in mind that God can also choose to *test you*.

God's rewards are not always the kind that fit inside an envelope or show up as adjustments to your bank statement. The true blessings of the Lord are the intangible ones: peace, joy, and contentment.

Following the Secret Sermon, Jesus reminds us that God's timetable for distributing rewards is not limited to our life on earth. These treasures extend into our life in heaven as well (see Matthew 6:20–21). In fact, the early church Christians were so hungry for God's future rewards that they were willing to endure further suffering to "gain a better resurrection." (Those aren't my words, by the way. For more, see Hebrews 11:35.)

Those who walk with God understand that giving generously doesn't mean a new business venture will succeed, that they will never be sick, or that their child will not stray from the faith. Neither are they shocked when a mind-boggling, buzzer-shot blessing falls from heaven, making them look up to catch God's gaze.

While financial rewards are common, they are not boomerang responses to every good deed. Most often God's rewards are experienced in the form of a general sense of peace and joy, experienced over a lifetime of giving. Givers caught up in the joy of giving don't always recognize when God's blessings are triggered. Sometimes it takes a year or more to put the pieces together and recognize the timing of one of God's rewards. And when this realization happens, that's God's way of saying, "See? I really do notice you."

Interested in a Connection?

I used to view financial giving as my responsibility to my church, to missionaries, and to the needy. But my rice-and-beans shopping experience with Mrs. Whyte helped me to see the bigger (and biblical) reason for giving. We give to connect with God, which in turn allows Him to connect with us.

Do you want to connect with God in this way? Do you want to be seen by Him? Maybe it's time to take some risks in this area. It may be time to step out and reach toward heaven with things you hold on to tightly: your money and possessions.

If you are not giving to God, then now's the time to start. If you have been giving when it's convenient or only when it's comfortable to do so, it's time for you to begin giving serious gifts. If you've been wondering why your walk with God feels stale, perhaps it's because your giving pattern is, too.

Giving is the first of the three ingredients Jesus points out in His Secret Sermon. He wants us to understand how pivotal giving can be to jump-start our walk with God. Just as Jesus noticed the widow in the Temple who gave so generously, He notices us when we give.

When I told Mrs. Whyte to give from her twenty dollars and her rice and beans, I really believed what I said: *"Jesus will see it, He will be pleased, and He will reward you."*

Still, for some time after that encounter, I wondered if my words to her were appropriate. Ultimately I concluded that even if the words felt strange to speak, they lined up with the message of the prophet John... and Jesus.

If you get serious about your gifts to God, He will see it. And He will let you know that He sees it.

And when that happens, you will hear His divine applause.

10

Spiritual Hearing Loss

If seeing an invisible God is complicated, so is hearing Him…at least for me. It's because I have spiritual hearing loss.

For years I heard pastors and television preachers say things such as "God spoke to me…" and "I heard God say to me…" I kept wondering if they got to hear God speak with an audible voice. Or were they getting a message from God that only they could hear?

Some of them talked in other ways about hearing God, saying, "God led me…," "God prompted me…," "I sensed God's Spirit…" This type of hearing made more sense to me, but still I was fuzzy on how it worked.

No matter how we define *hearing God,* we all suffer from some degree of spiritual hearing loss. Not only is God invisible, He is also mostly inaudible. Just as we need to learn how to see Him in ways that don't involve eyesight, we need to be able to hear Him in ways that don't rely on the sound of His voice. For most of us, that means we're listening for something that *feels* like God's voice.

When We Don't Hear

Having a physical hearing loss has always been difficult for me. Even when I have my bionic devices powered up, I miss much of what is being heard by others.

When I can't hear, I feel separated from what's going on. If I'm watching a movie with my family and struggle to hear, I become disconnected from the experience. As I become disconnected, I begin to lose focus. I often begin to daydream or drift off to sleep. Or I may get out my laptop and focus on my work or do some reading. I gravitate toward something I can "hear."

When you don't hear God, you feel disconnected spiritually. Bible study doesn't do much for you. Quiet times feel like a waste of time. Prayer seems pointless.

As you disconnect spiritually, you fall prey to a lack of direction, purpose, and focus in your life of faith. Then discouragement sets in. You become discouraged with your church, your small group, and with other ministry and fellowship opportunities. You might even blame your disconnectedness on the failings of other people. But the cause of your dissatisfaction may well be that you don't hear God.

When you can't hear God, you are likely to start pouring time and energy into things you *can* hear. It might be playing golf, fishing, or hunting. It could be watching television or college football, checking out social media, shopping online, or playing video games. It could even be the seemingly good things—like your job, your studies, and even busy church work that crowds the focus needed to hear God's voice.

When I struggle to hear physically, questions crowd my mind: *What did they say? What did they mean? Did they ask me to do something, to help with something?* The same sort of thing happens when we can't hear spiritually, except the questions have a greater bearing on our souls. They sound like this:

- Does anyone really hear God?
- Does God even speak to people today?
- Why does God remain distant and aloof?
- Is God there?
- Is God even real?

Many have checked out of the faith because of the simple fact that they can't hear God.

What Are "Ears to Hear"?

"But blessed are your eyes because they see, and your ears because they hear." (Matthew 13:16)

When Jesus talked about having eyes to see and ears to hear, He was talking about spiritual senses. He said, "He who belongs to God hears what God says" (John 8:47).

This could cause you to question whether you belong to God, especially if you think Jesus meant hearing God like you'd hear a weather report on the radio. If Jesus was referring to audible messages, then I'm in real trouble. I would guess you are too.

So what does it mean to have ears to hear?

As I have lived with hearing loss, I've learned ways to hear differently. Interestingly, the same things I do to hear physically are some of the things we all can do to hear spiritually.

Choose to Hear

In college I decided to take my hearing disability more seriously. I had squandered too many years choosing not to hear others. Now I was motivated to try harder. The consequences of not succeeding in college meant my chances of finding a good job would be limited. I needed to hear everything I could possibly hear.

As much as I resented the battery-powered devices, I put them back in my ears. Even with hearing aids, though, my hearing is far from perfect. I still miss out on so much.

As a hearing-impaired person, I have to choose to hear. It's an active process, an intentional act. I have to tune in my listening ears and decide to hear. My children, who have perfect hearing, can choose to halfway pay attention yet still follow a conversation pretty well. I have to be all in. If I tune out, I'm disconnected.

When I try to hear, I may be able to catch two, three, or four out of five words. If I lose focus or choose to listen less, I might hear just one word—or none.

The same intentional focus is needed as we listen for God. Most Christians are spiritually hearing-impaired because they choose not to hear. On one level, they may want to hear God. But they don't want to put in the effort, so they miss most or all of what God is saying to them.

Instead, people are happy to go about their busy lives—often including a number of church or ministry commitments—but they never fully tune in to hear God. I am an expert at doing churchy stuff and proclaiming Christian values, but I'm not very good at choosing to hear God. At times I find myself doing everything except trying to hear God because I'm living a distracted Christian life.

But deep inside I want the full experience, a real relationship with God. It takes an intentional shift to hear God. And as Samuel demonstrated, it starts with a few simple words to God: "Speak, for your servant is listening" (1 Samuel 3:10).

Of course not all of us get to hear the audible voice of God calling to us, as Samuel did. So what are the things we must do once we choose to hear?

Go to God's Voice

Homes for those with a physical disability are designed with wheelchair ramps and wide door openings. The visually impaired have megasized TV screens and jumbo digital alarm clocks. But at my house, my family treats me like I can hear perfectly. It's mainly my fault; that is how I have trained them. All my life I have worked to get close to the voice in order to hear what is being said.

When my kids yell my name, I run into the other room so I can hear them. When Stephanie calls from upstairs, I come out of my office to hear what she is saying. When my neighbor calls out from a distance, I hear noise but not words. So I begin moving in the direction of the noise. I read lips, so getting closer to the voice is helpful.

Hearing God is the same. We have to move toward His voice. Jesus is our best model for this practice. "Very early in the morning, while it was still dark, Jesus got up, left the house and went off to a solitary place, where he prayed" (Mark 1:35). Jesus understood the need to go toward the voice of His Father. He capitalized on the quiet of the early morning hours, knowing that is when He could be alone with God, free of distractions and noise.

King David sought comfort in a morning routine of going before God, seeking His voice: "But I cry to you for help, O Lord; in the morning my prayer comes before you" (Psalm 88:13).

Of course, there is no rule that requires you to meet with God in the morning. You can meet with Him in the morning, afternoon, evening— whenever. I know, however, that if I don't set aside time in the morning, it likely will not happen later in the day. Once the day kicks off, the kids are up, carpools begin, then come the workday, e-mails, lunch meetings, conference calls.

And what about getting alone? Do you have to be closed up in a prayer closet or behind a locked door in your office in order to hear God? Actually, Jesus said a prayer closet is not a bad idea (see Matthew 6:6). But He didn't make it a requirement.

There is one requirement, however, when it comes to prayer. It's that you do it. In the Secret Sermon, Jesus does not say *if* you pray, He says *"when* you pray" (Matthew 6:5). If you seek a connection with God and want to hear His voice, getting to a place by yourself—at a time when you won't be distracted—has to be a "when."

Prayer is your secret ingredient. It always will be easier to turn on the TV, pick up your laptop or tablet or cell phone, or do just about anything else. But God is looking to meet with you privately, where secrets are shared.

Hearing God requires initiative, planning, and action. You have to undertake the necessary preparations. This may involve going to bed earlier so you can get out of bed sooner, scheduling a weekend retreat away so you can be alone, or skipping some lunches with colleagues to spend time in prayer. Hearing God demands movement to a place where it's just you and God—no one else and nothing else.

Master the Text

In college, I'd make a point to meet with my professors at the beginning of each semester. I particularly wanted to know what percentage of the test questions were based on assigned reading and how many were based on classroom lectures and discussion. This helped me gauge how important it was to hear in class, since hearing requires extra work for me.

I learned to excel in the classroom by studying textbooks. Even if I missed some of the spoken words, the written words were what I really needed. In similar ways, we can't hear God apart from His text. We must set our eyes on His written words, the Bible.

Read the Bible. Radical insight, isn't it?

I know you've heard that advice so many times it likely has lost its impact. So let's look at this another way. When I was in college, I wasn't studying textbooks to check off items on my to-do list. I wanted to learn and grow so I could take the next steps in my journey—which would bring me closer to my career goals. The rewards and the "why" change everything. Reading God's text takes you deeper in your spiritual journey, leading you closer to God. When you think about it, the Bible is the only tangible expression of God Himself. While God is invisible, His Word is something we can feel, see, and hear. (It's even on a phone app.)

If you want to connect with God, you can't ignore His text. And I'm not talking about dusting off your failed Bible-reading plan and trying harder this time. I'm talking about approaching the Bible with a fresh expectancy. As you turn to the first page, ask God for eyes that see and ears that hear.

This involves taking greater risks in today's Christian culture. Reading and feasting on God's text seems to be falling out of favor. Knowing just enough to dismiss what you don't want to believe is growing more popular.

Seeking to hear God through His Word will require you to think deeply about your own beliefs and society's growing intolerance of this book.

It's okay to have questions, even big questions, about passages of Scripture. But like many things in life, our attitude toward something determines what we get out of it. If you've made up your mind that the Bible isn't relevant, you might fit in with the culture, but you'll miss out on a walk with God. It takes guts to accept God's mysteries expressed on those pages. False intellectualizing is the fastest way to slow your walk to a crawl...and then to a retreat away from God.

It's not about swallowing and regurgitating certain passages with mindless resolve. But the more you digest the text—in it's fullness and with an open heart—the more you will begin to see things from God's perspective. Mastering the text is part of the steady, plodding process of seeking God, learning to discern His voice, and encountering Him through His written words.

And remember, just as going to God in prayer does not always get a message in return, reading God's text does not always mean words will jump off the page. But over time you will begin to know His voice because you know His ways more clearly—by knowing the text.

What God Is Seeing

> God looks down from heaven on the sons of men to see if there
> are any who understand, any who seek God. (Psalm 53:2)

When I get out of bed in the dark hours and head to my home office or to the living room to pray, I feel like I'm doing the right things to hear from God. But often, what I experience is nothing. It's dark; the house is cold; it's quiet. Plus, I'm sleepy.

I may get down on my knees or plop into a chair and start to pray. Or I may pull out my Bible and turn to a page. Often I start to fall asleep or become distracted, so I get up to move around. But then I decide to check e-mail. Or I might look out a window to check the weather.

Next thing I know I start thinking about my day, and then I'm right back into the daily routine of work, clutter, and demands…and away from my time with God.

On a day such as that, I started out by going toward the voice and putting myself in a position to hear God. But doing so does not guarantee a daily report from heaven. It simply means that you get as close as you can to a place where God notices your desire to be noticed by Him.

Often, going toward the voice is more about showing God you're trying to hear than it is about actually hearing. Hearing God starts with your showing God you want to hear, even if it seems as if you don't hear a thing.

If my earthly father could find joy in watching me hit a golf ball off a tee, how much more pleasure does my Heavenly Father receive when He watches me seek His voice? When God looks down and notices His son, Jeffrey, He sees a child seeking Someone he can't see or hear. When I move toward the voice, showing my desire to hear God, it gets God's attention. God likes it when He sees my faith in action.

Daniel had been praying and fasting when an angel appeared to tell him God had been listening (see Daniel 9:20–23). Cornelius was in one of his afternoon prayer sessions when an angel tapped him on the shoulder with a similar message: God had been listening (see Acts 10:30–31).

You may not get a visit from an angel. But try picturing God's eyes gazing at you as you go toward the voice. It will remind you that the invisible God is watching.

After seeking God earnestly, you will have that special moment when silence is broken. And you'll hear His applause.

Call-Out Moments

Your father knows what you need before you ask him. (Matthew 6:8)

When Abraham's servant Steve threw out a buzzer-shot request to God, it was a silent prayer in his heart (see Genesis 24:45). When I was praying from the bleachers, I did so silently in my heart. While it would be nice to hear from God audibly, He does not need to hear us audibly. God knows our thoughts before we even ask. He's tracking us that closely (see Psalm 139:2).

However, sometimes God's patience in responding can cause you to wonder if your silent prayers (or even spoken ones) are flawed or lacking. God might be waiting until He sees that you are desperate to hear. Sometimes He waits for you to yell.

God knows when you are deeply frustrated, wondering why with all the talk about hearing God you don't hear a word. He is particularly interested in knowing that you are turning to Him, moving toward His voice, being intentional, making a sincere effort.

I have been desperate to hear God's voice. At those times I have called out to Him (okay, screamed) while driving. I have scribbled desperate messages in my journal. I've looked up to the heavens in despair, wondering why God was ignoring me.

Years ago, Stephanie and I were wrestling with a career decision. We prayed and we prayed. We looked to God for the next steps, but we heard nothing. One day I was driving through town…and I screamed out to God. I guess you could call it a prayer—or maybe a form of holy road rage.

I released months of frustration in a short tirade. I shared my heavy heart. Of course, God already knew (see Matthew 6:8), but it felt good to express the pain and confusion I felt as a result of His silence.

A few months later I received a buzzer-shot answer, and I could trace it back to the holy road-rage incident. I'm not saying yelling is the best way to be heard. I did not insist that God conform to my timetable or that He appear on demand. Rather I opened my heart; I shared the rawness of my soul. I expressed the authentic cries of a child desperately seeking the attention of my Father.

God knows when you are desperate to be noticed. He is particularly interested in knowing that you're turning to Him, not as a matter of habit or convenience, but because you need with all your being to be heard and to hear back from Him. God knows when you have reached a breaking point and are now in a position to hear His answer.

During the Secret Sermon, Jesus taught the disciples to pray a simple prayer (see Matthew 6:9–13). It is known as the Lord's Prayer. The first two words, "Our Father," are my favorite part. That's how we all begin to call out to our Father: by addressing Him. From there, just let it flow.

Writing Thoughts to God

Sometimes we don't see God's response to our prayers because we're behaving like children—easily distracted and drawn away by other interests.

Like all parents, Stephanie and I do things for our kids all the time. They often are oblivious to the little things we do for them, and depending on their age, they can't even comprehend the bigger things. But as they mature, they see more. And they appreciate more.

Growing up spiritually takes time. But there are steps we can take that help us grow faster and catch more of what God is doing for, in, and around us. One of these ways is to journal our prayers—writing notes to God.

I've journaled thoughts and prayers to God for more than fifteen years. It's amazing how much you can see when you write it down. If I hadn't recorded my prayers, many of my encounters of hearing and seeing God would have vaporized. I would have forgotten the encounters or missed them completely.

When my young children give me stick-figure art to display on the refrigerator or a birthday note telling me "you're the best dad ever," it tugs at my heart. I envision God having a similar reaction from my notes to Him.

Hearing Secrets

Hearing God is a lot like hearing a spouse, a friend, or anyone else with whom you share a close relationship. You don't always have to hear their voice to know what they mean. Stephanie can give me a look and I know immediately if she is pleased with me, impatient with me, being playful, wanting my attention, or ready to have a meltdown. As you choose to hear God and take steps toward His voice, you'll hear Him in ways that don't require audible sounds.

God's voice is not always crystal clear, so you need to learn to listen in faith and act in faith. This involves taking chances, acting on what you think you heard. I didn't hear a clear voice telling me to stop by the grocery store to find the salon visitor. But Mrs. Whyte was there, searching for rice and beans. When I walked the aisles asking God for words to share, there were no voices then either.

Often God is initiating a journey that He wants you to take with Him. It might not make sense to you at the start. Like driving in fog at night, you can see only to the far end of your headlight beams. But as you follow the light, you continue to make progress. It might be slow and uncertain, but you are moving forward. In the same way, the more you learn to trust the voice of God, the more ready you will be when you hear Him the next time, and the next. You will be further down the road in your relationship with Him.

When you encounter God's voice, it is an opportunity to deepen your relationship, in secret. Just you and God—in your prayer closet, while screaming your need, or wherever you are when you go toward His voice.

The verse you stumbled upon in your early morning quiet time and later heard again in your pastor's sermon may mean much to you, but very little to someone else. The unexpected phone call you receive after a desperate cry to God might sound like God's voice to you, but to others it is nothing but coincidence.

That's why cultivating secrets is so important as you begin to hear God's voice. Like wine that enriches over time, these secrets will increase in value the longer you hold them in your heart.

As you gain confidence in hearing God, you'll experience breakouts in your faith. They may be breakouts that propel your life forward in visible ways, such as a new career path, a new ministry calling, meeting a spouse, or adopting a child. Or you might experience inner breakouts that strengthen your soul: receiving specific revelation as you read God's words, overcoming a personal insecurity, accepting God's forgiveness, or simply being reminded of God's presence in a very real way.

A secret encounter with God can confirm, beyond doubts and insecurity, the one thing you long to know: that God sees you.

11

Waiting to Be Seen

It was Cade's turn to have breakfast with Dad. Our Friday-morning routine involved an outing for me and one of my three boys. Cade's favorite breakfast spot was a bagel shop.

On this day, though, I suggested a slight change of plan. I would go out to pick up bagels for the family, rather than Cade and I going to have bagels at the shop. My sleepy-headed five-year-old nodded his agreement. With everyone else still in bed, I sat Cade on the couch in our upstairs master bedroom. The window overlooked the driveway so he could see me when I came back with a box of bagels.

He buried his head in his blanket while I slipped out the bedroom door.

Twenty minutes later I returned home. It was still early so I cut up the bagels, set out juice, and prepared the table. Then I went upstairs to get Cade, since he wanted to share the surprise with the family.

Stephanie was still asleep, but Cade was not on the couch in our bedroom. I went to the boys' bedroom, but Cade was not there either. Thinking I must have missed him while setting up the bagel buffet, I went back downstairs. Still, no Cade.

Figuring one more house check was in order before I woke up Momma, I then searched each room (and closet!), even looking under beds. He was nowhere to be found.

By now, mild panic had set in. I woke up Stephanie and gave her my best "Don't freak out" story.

It was not effective.

Faster than you can say "bagel," she was out of bed and racing through the house. "What do you mean he's gone?" My wobbly parental esteem took another dip.

Then we noticed the front door had been opened. Out the door we went. We circled the house. My wife ran one way, I the other. We met in the backyard and then returned to the front. Stephanie was screaming Cade's name.

Waking up the neighbors was not a concern at this point; we were in red-alert mode.

We expanded the search perimeter to the surrounding streets, with Stephanie going west and me to the east. In a few seconds, Stephanie switched to calling out *my* name, so I turned to see what she was pointing to. At the end of the block, a small child was walking toward us, holding the hand of a stranger.

Out of Bounds

We took off in their direction. In a moment, Cade was quickly swallowed up in Stephanie's arms. I arrived a few seconds later with a slightly cooler stride. (One of us needed to fake a responsible-parent appearance!)

Cade was dressed in pajamas and snow boots. It was a precious and ridiculous sight. We convinced the kind stranger (or I should say we tried) that we were the rightful parents. I asked where he found our son.

"I was driving by and saw him sitting on the big rock at the neighborhood entrance," the man answered.

That was *way* outside Cade's boundaries.

Cade had headed out our front door, went down our street, made a turn onto another street, then walked down that street, then crossed a street, and then headed down another. He covered nearly four blocks before he reached the neighborhood entrance. What in the world was he thinking?

I could only imagine what the good Samaritan thought about these two frantic parents who had allowed their child to slip out of their home, alone, so early in the morning. I began to get an idea as we turned to go into our house and two police cars pulled up. The good Samaritan must have turned us in. (I don't blame him.)

We invited two uniformed men into our home. On the living room couch sat our other two boys, who were oblivious to the drama. The oldest one wondered why we invited cops over for breakfast.

Next to them was their back-to-normal-blood-pressure momma. Across the room in the love seat was a bewildered dad. Next to me was the prime suspect, Cade, the runaway child.

The officers assessed the situation and my goofy story that went with it. They saw the bagels and juice on the table and determined it was all right to leave. I'm thankful they didn't seize our breakfast as evidence.

Interrogation

Before the officers left, they asked if they could have a chat with the runaway. Standing directly in front of Cade, they did their best to communicate to a five-year-old that what he did was a dangerous thing. Cade didn't fully get it. But he remained silent until the officers drove off.

I huddled our family together, then turned my attention to Cade.

"Why did you leave the house?"

His answer, "I went to find you."

"Why did you go all the way to the edge of the neighborhood?"

"Because I knew you would see me there."

"How did you know Daddy would see you?"

"You always drive by that big rock. I knew you would see me, Dad."
He repeated the phrase a few more times, indicating his confidence in his
father seeing him waiting on the rock.

My heart slipped down to my stomach.

Most of the time, Cade's expectation would have been right on the
money. Usually we pass the rock on our way in or out of the neighborhood. I would not have missed my strangely outfitted boy sitting on a
boulder waiting for my return. But our neighborhood has multiple en-
trances, and that morning I took another route. I didn't see Cade, and he
didn't see me.

Our emotions gradually settled, and the breakfast of bagels helped
put the family at ease. Eventually I realized how endearing this picture
was.

In Cade's childlike way, he went to the edge of his world—walking
way outside his boundaries. He was there waiting for his daddy to see
him. He never feared. He never doubted. He just waited calmly and fully
expected to be seen.

I thought about his faith. It's the kind of faith God desires of us, that
we would know He sees us and that we would be eager to travel outside
our safety zone to be noticed by Him.

Have you ever wanted to be like my son Cade? Just to sit on a rock
next to a place where you know God passes by, then wait until your
Father notices you?

Beyond Bagels

I treasure my bagel sessions with Cade, pancakes with Gunnar, and donuts with little Autumn. I enjoy eating ribs with Austin. Stephanie and I

enjoy our special Italian restaurant. And I have fond boyhood memories of eating pizza with my family on Saturday nights. Few things are as enjoyable as eating with people you love.

You may notice how certain relationships are marked by special meals. It's what makes the picture of the Last Supper so touching. Have you ever considered that many of the revealing stories shared in the Gospels were told around meals? I imagine the disciples looked forward to their meals with Jesus, who would sit with them and unpack more teachings, more stories, more secrets.

God enjoys watching His children feast. Three times a year the Israelites assembled for a time of feasting, celebration, and worship. Consider the items they offered on the altar: steak, bread, wine. While God's glory consumed His share on the altar, His children were partaking in their share. The items that were sacrificed had deeply symbolic implications; they also served a practical purpose: feasting.

But there's another kind of meal that God treasures with His children. I think of it as *the fast meal*. It's very filling for God and can be for us as well.

Fasting? No Thanks!

I love buffets, going back for seconds, any opportunity to indulge my appetite. That's why the idea of fasting—going without food—at first seemed ridiculous to me. The only thing I like about being hungry is that it reminds me it's time to eat.

Say what you will about fasting—when you choose to eat less, or not at all—it gets your attention. And when you do things that get your own attention, they can also get God's attention. Fasting is one of the secret ingredients that Jesus mentioned in His Secret Sermon. Without question, it is one of the things God notices.

After fasting forty days and forty nights, Jesus was hungry (see Matthew 4:2). That's well over a month without food. If I go forty *minutes* without food, I'm already hungry again. If I skip lunch, then I'll *really* be hungry. And if I skip dinner too? Good grief!

Logic says the longer you go without food, the hungrier you'll feel. But logic doesn't seem to apply to fasting. While hunger remains noticeable for the first several days, there is a point at which the feeling of hunger dies down. After a few days without food, the stomach quits growling, the hunger pangs soften, and you realize you're not going to die for lack of bagels.

You start feeling better, not worse. Sounds backward, I know. That's because God made the human body to fast. Maybe that's why Jesus said during the Secret Sermon, "*When* you fast" (Matthew 6:16). Since we can fast, He assumes that we will.

God provided one day a week for us to rest from activity. For the land of Israel, He provided one year out of seven for resting the soil. It makes sense that God would have a mechanism for resting the stomach too. The problem is the mind still wants to eat. Food not only feeds us physically but emotionally too.

If you're having a rough day, a good meal can lift the spirits. After a difficult week in the office, a Friday-night dinner with friends or family can salvage frayed emotions. Even simple meals such as early morning coffee, a midmorning snack, or an afternoon trip to the vending machine all provide a spark.

In our Western context where food is abundant, we depend on food for comfort and enjoyment, even entertainment. That's one reason why after eating, even though physical hunger fades, the mind still might crave dessert. During a fast, the body may not crave food, but the brain does. And therein lies the secret about fasting.

God made the body to endure fasting from food so the mind could relax its fixation on physical food and feast on spiritual food instead. The body will be fine. And the mind will too, if we allow it. God wants us to feast with Him while fasting from food.

Another Muffin, Please

I enjoy meeting with friends at a coffee shop to talk about God while eating a muffin and sipping a hot drink. And what's a small-group meeting without a large bowl of chips or a mini buffet of sweets?

There's nothing wrong with food-friendly gatherings. But God relishes times when we set aside the desires of our stomachs and talk *to* Him alone, rather than being satisfied to talk *about* Him with others.

It's not surprising that fasting raises questions. Why does fasting please God? Why does our discomfort due to a lack of food comfort Him? Why is our emptiness so filling to Him?

As you fast you will be hungry. When you are hungry, you find yourself seeking something else to replace the pleasure and comfort that comes from physical food. That "something else" is prayer! As you are reminded of your hunger, you'll pray more intently, reflect on God more frequently, desire the comfort of the Scriptures more authentically. When you fast, you replace physical nourishment with spiritual nourishment.

Fasting tells the body and the mind who's boss, and it puts you in a position to desire God and connect with Him more. God takes pleasure in that! After all, who wants to be bossed around by a donut? Really. You're made for bigger things.

We fast as a way to draw nearer to God than is possible when we are distracted by earthly concerns, such as catering to our hunger. We fast to remove obstacles. Bottom line: we fast because we want more life in our lives! We fast, believing in what we can't see, trusting that God is taking notice and is pleased when we do this.

It is a lot like a young child venturing out of the house to walk four blocks, then sit alone on a rock, waiting until he is seen by his father. In the same way, fasting puts you in the direct view of God.

First Steps

Sometimes we fast simply to draw closer *to* God. Moses fasted for forty days seeking an encounter on a mountain. At other times we fast because we desperately need something *from* God. Esther and the Israelites fasted three days seeking God's intervention so they could escape the deadly plotting of Haman. Daniel fasted twenty-one days seeking God's forgiveness for his people.

No need to worry about the difference. Both approaches can be pleasing to Him.

Have you ever sensed God calling you to a different path in life? Or maybe you need to make a life-altering decision, such as choosing the best form of medical treatment, proposing marriage, investing in a new business, sending a child off to college.

Years ago I was facing a decision that would affect my career and family in significant ways. I wanted to hear from God and to be absolutely sure of His direction. I was craving peace and clarity, so I decided to fast.

For a brief season I fasted from food one day a week. Some days I sensed God's favor and pleasure. Important phone calls connected easily, e-mails I had waited for were returned, and yes, my stomach reminded me to seek out secret times with God.

But other fast days were far different—I would experience just another busy day, grinding out my routine until breakfast the next day, when I would eat again. At times, my hunger made me irritable. I didn't feel like fasting, but I didn't want to quit either. Hunger, determination, and curiosity can bring about good things.

Week after week I stumbled around with the one-day-per-week fasting schedule, hoping, trusting, and believing that God would take notice of my giving up food for twenty-four hours.

Several months into my one-day fast routine, God gave me the clarity I needed for my situation. Peace replaced angst and confidence replaced my fears. More importantly, I experienced a fresh connection to God. It was a breakout for my faith.

Ceaseless Connection

Fasting is a form of continuous prayer. During a fast, every hour (or minute, it seems) your stomach is asking the brain: "Hey, why aren't you feeding me?"

Your brain responds, "Chill! I'm fasting."

Then the stomach asks, "Fasting? What for?"

"To draw near to God."

Sometimes the stomach will respond with something like, "That's nuts… You know, a few almonds would really hit the spot right about now."

As you are reminded constantly of the food you are not eating, thoughts turn to God in the form of prayer. I believe God wants everyone to fast in some way. Whether it be fasting for a day or simply a meal (or in other ways that fit one's abilities and particular health situation), fasting is effective at getting God's attention because it captures *our* full attention. Fasting helps turbocharge your prayers, both in frequency and in intensity.

Fasting is a mental battle where the mind wages war with the flesh.

Ultimately, it makes sense under only one condition: you believe an invisible God sees you, is pleased, and will reward you.

Zero Bytes

In a home with four children, technology is a big deal. It's a big distraction too. If I want to get my child's attention, I impound his or her iPhone, iPad, or any other iSomething.

It's amazing how much of an impact removing these things has on my children and our relationship. The tech void leads to renewed involvement in areas of living that matter more. They talk with their siblings, answer Mom's and Dad's questions more completely, hang out in the family room, and participate in conversations in the car.

That's the power fasting has for our lives. Fasting helps to restore balance. It's a calibrating tool that reprograms our focus, sharpening our connection with an invisible God.

Bigger Steps and Bigger Tests

After my experiment with single-day fasting, I sensed God was motioning to me to come closer. I also was facing new life situations that demanded extra clarity. My faith was being stretched. Remember, each encounter with God means new tests lie ahead. That's when I began to explore longer fasts.

Fasting is my way of letting God know that I am well aware of my limits. It's my way of telling God that I desire more of His attention, His strength, and His favor.

Unfortunately, fasting often is misunderstood. For a lot of us, myself included, food can play too large a role in our existence. Television networks are devoted to looking at, preparing, and talking about food. Food is an idol in our affluent Western world. People wonder why anyone would go a day, three days, or seven days or more without food.

It reminds me of the question I had for Cade:

"Why did you go all the way to the edge of the neighborhood?"

"Because I knew you would see me there."

The reason I fast is the same reason Cade found the boulder and sat patiently, waiting for me to come by. I believe that when I fast, God will see me waiting for Him to pass by.

If I get in a quiet place, then sit and wait, I'll see Him more clearly. And I'll notice His noticing me more clearly too.

Not So Fast

The time will come when the bridegroom will be taken from them; then they will fast. (Matthew 9:15)

When the Pharisees asked Jesus why His disciples didn't fast, He said they didn't need to. They already were with Him and didn't need to fast to draw near to Him.

If Jesus came to earth to spend a day with you, giving you His full attention, would you fast? Of course not. You would feast with Him. You would drive around saying, "Jesus, where do You want to eat?" And He might say, "Wherever you want to eat."

Or maybe you'd choose to cook Him a meal. You might propose steak, and He might suggest grilling fish instead, just as He did with His fishing buddies (see John 21). But you would have His full attention, and He would have yours. Fasting would not be necessary!

Jesus told the Pharisees that His disciples would fast when He was away from them. Jesus knew the disciples would desire His attention after He ascended to the Father. Sure enough, after Jesus departed to heaven, the disciples fasted often.

You don't fast to impress God; you fast to be with Him. The Pharisees didn't understand this difference.

Some Rules for Fasting

You can fast for one meal, one day, five days, eighteen days, or longer. You can fast from all foods or certain foods. Some practice a partial fast by eating only fresh fruits and vegetables. Juicing—drinking only fresh fruit and vegetable juices while abstaining from solid foods—is common as well. Juicing allows nutrients into the system and helps slow weight loss over an extended period of fasting.

Without a doubt, fasting involves sacrifice. That's one way it focuses our hearts and eyes. However, the idea is not to flex your muscles and show God how tough you are. Rather, the point is to put the body and mind in position to focus on God in more concentrated ways.

Even children can fast with the family in appropriate ways. One summer day Stephanie led our four children in a twelve-hour fast in which they ate just fresh fruits and vegetables. (I know, this is the normal diet for some families, but for carb-hungry Andersons, it was a big deal!) She led them in a brief time of prayer and Scripture reading at the top of each hour.

We capped off the family experience with a celebration dinner. And let me tell you, they feasted like little kings and a queen. Never had they longed for a meal as they did that day. And never had they focused on God so intently. It was an experience that will stay with them.

There are many ways to fast. The main rule is that there are no rules.

Fasting is for you! There are some best practices that can help you in your fasting journey, and I share more details at DivineApplause.com.

Life Is More Than Food

Jesus asked, "Is not life more important than food?" (Matthew 6:25)

Jesus had just completed his forty-day fast in the desert when He preached His Sermon on the Mount. When Jesus declared that life is more important than food and clothes, He had a unique perspective on what this really meant. His journey had been a fresh reminder of a different kind of food.

In an inconceivable way, Jesus was God yet He was somewhat separated from the now-invisible Father. He desired whatever proximity He could have with God. He sensed the time was at hand for His ministry to begin, and it was a daunting mission. He would have just a few short years to ignite a discipleship movement that would follow Him to the cross.

Jesus knew that fasting was in order. He knew how much He needed God's attention and comfort, and the power that comes from this kind of seeking.

God desires to see you going out of your way to get in His front-and-center view. Fasting places you at the center of His attention—it's like going way outside your comfort zone to sit on a rock while waiting for God to pass by.

12

When God Passes By

I often think back to when Cade ventured out to that big rock. We don't live in the same neighborhood anymore, but occasionally I drive by our old house for memories' sake. From the car I'll retrace Cade's path to the neighborhood entrance, and I'll stop for a moment and stare at the rock. It's still there. Big rocks like those are not easily moved.

I still wonder how long five-year-old Cade would have waited at the rock if he had not been rescued. Thirty minutes? Two hours? How long would a little boy wait for his daddy to pass by?

Seeking More

Just over a year after I discovered fasting, God put me in the path of a few men who had completed a forty-day fast. At the time, I didn't know such a thing was possible. (Meaning Jeff-possible as opposed to Bible-possible.) And even if it was, the idea didn't seem like a healthy thing to put your body through. But these men were still kicking, so I had to reconsider.

Desiring more in my journey with God, I prayed about whether this was a walk God might have in mind for me. I sensed it was, so I jumped in.

I launched my fast during a business trip, which complicated my commitment. Traveling was typically a chance to stop for a big juicy steak. Every billboard seemed to be advertising one…and those ads were testing my resolve! But I continued to press on.

If you fast for an extended period of time, say from seven to twenty days, it likely will overlap with special occasions. There's bound to be a holiday, birthday, or special meal opportunity somewhere along the way. Days twelve through fifteen of my extended fast kicked off a four-day stretch consisting of two family birthday parties, a Fourth of July church picnic, and a family cookout. The gatherings involved pizza, barbecued ribs, hamburgers, and birthday cake. (I *love* birthday cake.)

With each passing meal, I knew the fast was building value. When a plate of ribs passed in front of me, I expected God was noticing too. (He favors smoky meats, you know.) When cake and ice cream were being served, all I could envision was sitting on that rock, watching God watching me. It was a difficult four-day stretch.

When the spirit and the flesh are at odds, you know it. The spirit is trying to engage with God. The flesh wants to engage with a plate of ribs. Meanwhile, God is engaging with you. Really. His face is beaming as He gazes on you. That's what is happening, even if you don't sense His applause at the time.

Confidence and Doubt

A few days following my meat-free Fourth of July weekend, I finished the third week of the fast. After twenty-one days, the idea of a forty-day journey was feeling more attainable. At times it seemed like the longer the fast, the better my body felt. I had forgotten what it was like to be physically hungry. Believe me, I wanted to eat. But that was my mind talking, not my stomach.

Fasting brings great moments of clarity, confidence, and cleansing. During a fast your mind is open and alert. You read the Bible with greater intensity. Perspectives and priorities seem to get righted. Convictions cut deeper into your soul.

Strangely, though, fasting also can bring moments of doubt and insecurity. Fasting is a solo endeavor, a private journey. And because God is invisible and inaudible, your faith will be tested. (Think of Jesus being tempted while fasting in the desert.)

The longer the fast, the more you disengage from people (who, of course, are visible), and the more you try to engage with God, whom you can't see. Fasting forces you to deny many of the things that are visible—food, people, entertainment—and embrace what is invisible.

It's another paradox of fasting.

I had my moments of weakness, beginning with the nagging suspicion that maybe God was not noticing me. I wondered if my prayers were being heard. As the opposing feelings of confidence and doubt swirled in my mind, I chose a response that relies on faith. I deeply believed God notices when His children fast, and I wanted to be noticed. I chose to believe I was on the path God had paved for me and that He was watching.

Are You Pleased with Me?

Something about drawing close to God also brings us closer to our insecurities. Consider Moses. The closer he was to God, the more fragile he seemed.

Moses was chosen to stand up to Pharaoh and lead the Israelites out of Egypt. He was allowed to go into the tabernacle to meet with God alone. When Moses entered the tent, a pillar of cloud descended while God talked to him. Moses also was the one to go up on the mountain to receive the Ten Commandments from God.

Scriptures say God "would speak to Moses face to face, as a man speaks with his friend" (Exodus 33:11). How can a person be any closer to God than that? But the closer Moses drew to God, the more he longed for God's presence. The more he longed for God's presence, the more he longed for something else: God's affirmation.

Moses said: "If you are *pleased* with me, teach me your ways so I may know you and continue to find favor with you" (Exodus 33:13). Whatever goodness Moses felt from God, he wanted more of it. Despite the backstage access he enjoyed, he still needed to know God was pleased with him.

How could the man who stood up to the world's most powerful leader, the Pharaoh, be so insecure? Could it be the wounds he experienced from growing up in the palace, away from his real family? Or maybe his past sins still weighed on his conscience (killing a man would haunt me, too). Or was it the simple fact that the closer he drew to God, the lonelier he felt among others? Whatever it was, Moses longed for a greater connection to God.

Don't we all?

Invisible

My three weeks of fasting turned to four weeks. In the mornings I felt fantastic. Each day brought new energy, and a glass of juice did wonders too. But by day's end, I'd feel weak, tired, and ready for bed. When morning came, I was energized again.

On the thirty-second day, Stephanie took the kids with her to visit relatives for the weekend, leaving me some time alone. During one evening, I got down on my knees and called out to God, "Do you see me, God? Do you even notice me?"

I trusted that He did. (*Trust* being the key word.) But by now I was empty. Not just my stomach, but my spirit seemed empty too. I wanted to be done with the fast, but I still felt something was missing. Like

Moses, I wanted more: proof of God's presence. It was a mix of stubbornness and desperation. I needed to feel God's pleasure in a special way—which is how I found myself chasing my Heavenly Father.

Jacob wrestled all night with an angel while insisting that he receive a blessing from God. I wanted my own encounter.

I didn't really know what to look for. Would I see a bright light, or have a vision or a special dream? Would I see a sign in the clouds? Maybe hear a voice? Or maybe it would just be a peaceful shift in my heart.

I wasn't launching a global ministry like Jesus. I wasn't seeking healing for a dying child, like King David. I wasn't going up a mountain to receive the commandments from God like Moses or warding off a holocaust of the Jews like Esther.

I was sitting on a rock, waiting for God to come by and see me. I just wanted to notice God noticing me.

Wanting More

Moses asked God if God was pleased with him. Immediately, Moses heard what must be the most affirming statement anyone can hear: "I will do the very thing you have asked, because I am *pleased* with you and I know you by name" (Exodus 33:17).

God gave him a double affirmative: "I will do what you have asked. And, oh, by the way, Moses, I'm doing this because I am pleased with you!" They were stunning words. But not nearly as shocking as what Moses said next.

"Now show me your glory" (Exodus 33:18).

People say it's not wise to get ahead of God. Apparently Moses never got the memo.

Moses wanted it all. He was on a roll, asking for God's favor and getting it. But that wasn't enough. He wanted to be face to face with God!

God seemed pleased with his request, but there was a small problem. No human could see God's face or that person would die. As a consolation, God provided Moses a way to get as close as possible. God set an appointment for a meeting. The two would meet on a rock.

The Meeting Place

> Then the LORD said, "There is a place near me where you may
> stand on a rock." (Exodus 33:21)

Moses had been on this mountain before to meet with God. (He received two tablets bearing the commandments; later he hurled them off a cliff.) Now he would be headed up the hill for a second try.

God instructed Moses to stand in a certain place on the rock. "When my glory passes by, I will put you in a cleft in the rock and cover you with my hand until I have passed by. Then I will remove my hand and you will see my back; but my face must not be seen" (Exodus 33:22–23).

Let's not miss what's happening. Moses is aching to know that God is pleased with him. God answers in clear language, and in such a way that Moses is drawn into the moment and asks for more! Moses asks to see God's glory.

If God blasted my brain with the words "I'm delighted with you, Jeffrey," I'd probably melt right there on the spot. But I wonder if I'd let my soul's hunger loose in that moment and ask for more. Would I ask to see God? That's what Moses did.

Moses was so eager to be close to God and feel His pleasure that he made a bold request. If you are a parent, how would you feel if your child begged with such persistence for more time with you?

God Passed By

Moses went up on the mountain alone. He took two stone tablets with him, and he went to the rock as he was instructed. Then he waited. He was a patient man; he waited there forty days (again!). I suspect there wasn't much to eat or drink on the rock—no bagel shop, smoothie stand, or even a water fountain. God used supernatural means to keep him alive.

At some point during the forty-day wait, "the LORD came down in the cloud and stood there with him" (Exodus 34:5). And just as God had said He would, He passed by in front of Moses.

God was so close Moses could have reached out to touch Him. God was right there, shielding Moses from the stunning glory that would disintegrate his body. Moses's risk was rewarded, his hunger satisfied, and his deep longing was answered.

He wanted to see God, or at least as much of God as one could see and survive. He got his wish.

Bold Hunger

When you're on a fast, especially an extended one, you become bolder. You talk to God more candidly. You bare your soul more freely. The words in the Bible jump out at you and move you with greater conviction.

Fasting removes the guardrails that keep us in our comfort zones.

On the thirty-fourth day of my fast, a Saturday afternoon, I went to visit my great-aunt Katheryn. She was approaching her nineties and had been widowed and living alone for more than twenty years. She had no children, which magnified her loneliness. She did not know Jesus either. More loneliness.

My great-aunt was a sweet lady, but she had a crusty side and an iron will too. It seemed the older she became, the tougher she grew.

The purpose of my visit was to bring Jesus to the conversation. Outside of holidays and special family events, I had spent very little time with her. And I had never talked to her about Jesus. It seems easier to talk about Jesus with strangers and harder with family. I knew I'd never feel freer to take a risk than during a forty-day fast.

I spent twenty minutes or longer sharing with my great-aunt about the Good News. I started from the beginning—not with Adam but with Lucifer, an angel from heaven who walked away from God. Then I walked her through the Garden of Eden and continued the story to the Cross. I closed with a look at heaven and eternity. I did this as simply as I could.

Katheryn was quiet, and her questions were few. She did mention a television program she saw about a doctor talking about what happens to people when they die. The idea of heaven had not been part of her thinking. The idea of a deep sleep where you never wake up made more sense to her. My talk about sin and separation confused her. "I've been a good person," she said.

Performance-Enhancing Prayers

As I left Katheryn's house, I knew she was far from Jesus. But the seed had been planted. I rested in the fact that Katheryn's soul was in God's hands. When you fast, there's a greater peace about things you can't control. It's interesting how when I'm more tuned in to the flesh, I desire greater control of these things, not less.

Jesus told the disciples that some deeds can't be performed with prayer alone. Some things require prayer *and* fasting. Those are the things that require additional power and attention.

By faith, I trusted that my fast was working in Aunt Katheryn's corner, in whatever ways God works. As she tried to follow her great-nephew's ramblings, the only thing I could count on was that the secret fast might bring about the most significant reward in her life. I was trusting in the power of God's attention. I was standing on a rock holding a bright yellow sign that read, "Dear God, please notice my Aunt Katheryn."

Bittersweet

Day forty of the fast arrived. I was ready to return to normal activities. I had a list of favorite foods I couldn't wait to eat. For some reason fajitas ranked high on the list. So was a cheeseburger, peanut butter crackers, a chocolate chip cookie, a loaded baked potato, a handful of grapes...or even just one grape.

I looked forward to my first meal the next morning. An orange. Just a quarter of an orange. Never has the thought of a slice of fruit sounded so fulfilling.

I also was looking forward to engaging more with my family. The fasting experience creates a distance from others, which is a by-product of drawing nearer to God.

After my smallest-grocery-list-ever shopping trip, I drove across town to get a haircut. If this routine sounds a bit anticlimactic, it was.

During the fast, I had not experienced the God-encounter I had prayed for. But still I was at peace with my experience. I was reminded that faith is just that, trusting in what we can't see. We don't always get tangible proof of God's presence. King David must have felt that way when he fasted for seven days and his child died anyway. But his faith was not shaken.

If I had to do it over, would I? You bet. I'd do anything to show God that I'm much like a child, desiring to sit on a rock far outside my normal boundaries to wait for Him to come past.

And even without a direct encounter, fasting strengthened my resolve to follow my invisible God. Fasting gave me more time to pray for my wife and children, read and meditate on Scripture, journal my inner thoughts, examine my heart, experience times of solitude, marvel at the body's ability to endure a fast, conquer food's grip on my life. All of that was worth so much.

No, I didn't see God's hand to shield me from His face. I didn't see His backside...or even a toe. There were no voices or lights during my drive across town. But I did see something else.

God Winks

I was almost at the hair salon when I turned at an intersection and something caught my attention. I did a double take.

It was Mrs. Whyte! The lady who had gone out pushing a shopping cart, in search of rice and beans.

She was standing at the bus stop, the very one where we had said good-bye nearly two years earlier. Immediately I hit the brakes and made a hard right turn into the grocery store parking lot.

I had often thought about Mrs. Whyte. Was she staying warm in the winter? Was she getting food when she needed it? I especially remembered our conversation, and my suggestion to her that she share her cash (twenty dollars) and her rice and beans (the basics of her diet). Often I thought of what God might have been saying to me through those words.

She had no idea that our initial encounter had been, for me, like a grain of sand in an oyster. Our conversation continued to scratch around in me, bringing answers and more questions. The lessons I learned—that giving is for everyone and that God can be pleased by our gifts—continued to stir my heart.

And here she was at the bus stop, back in my path once again. I've never traveled through time before, but this moment sure felt like it.

Remember my saying how sometimes we take shots and the ball bounces around a bit before dropping through the hoop? Well this was one of those moments. I realized the shot I had taken, almost two years prior, was still in the air.

As I looked up, I saw God wink. Or it seemed like it. Like my earthly father when he stopped at the golf course on his way to work, peering at me as I lined up a tee shot. I could sense God's pleasure as He watched me pull into the grocery store parking lot, planning to say hello to Mrs. Whyte.

He had a secret surprise for me, and He had been waiting to share it for forty days.

And what was that surprise? Nothing short of the proof I had asked for: God notices me.

13

Walking with Doubt

I zoomed into the grocery store lot, parked, and jumped out of my car. I approached the bus stop and asked the woman who was waiting there: "Mrs. Whyte, do you remember me?"

She turned around and, as her eyes caught mine, the look on her face suggested she was as surprised as I was. And that she remembered me too!

"Oh yes," she said. "How is your baby?"

She had me stumped for a second. Then I remembered when we had met previously, I had told her about our new baby, Gunnar. I was impressed with her quick memory and touched by how she seemed to acknowledge me, as if we had talked just last week.

"The kids are great…they're growing up fast! How are you?"

We chatted for a few moments. Mrs. Whyte was a very simple lady and easy to talk to. There were no conversation barriers or protocols. I'd broken all those in our previous meeting when I suggested that she give from her meager possessions.

From our prior encounter, I knew she was in a housing transition. So I asked her where she lived, if she was keeping warm in the winter, and if she had food in the pantry. The basic things. I also asked about her furniture. She mentioned that she had a chair. I asked if she had a bed, and she told me she did not. When I asked where she slept, she said, "I sleep in my chair."

"It's a blue chair," she said. She seemed perplexed as to why I was so interested in the chair. I knew I'd be talking with her again, so I gave up on the questions. Since I had her address, I told her I'd visit. She seemed to welcome my offer.

Just like last time, the bus and its noisy brakes signaled an end to our conversation. I said good-bye and assured Mrs. Whyte that she'd see me soon.

Break-Fast

After my haircut, it was time to return home and prepare the next morning's breakfast. This consisted of selecting a blue-ribbon orange and setting it on the counter. No sense in peeling it yet. So I just stared at it.

I woke up early the next morning and went to the kitchen to get my meal. I peeled the orange, then pulled off a section and slowly chewed a small piece. It was the best orange I'd ever eaten.

This breakfast would give new meaning to the word *break-fast*. It had been forty days since I had had anything more than juice and water.

Over the next few days, I nibbled on different fruits and vegetables. It didn't take long, though, to wake up the system again. Before I knew it I was back to pizza, hamburgers, steak…and birthday cake.

Rearview Mirror

In the days following my fast, I reflected on the forty-day journey. My fast, chasing after God, my quest to be seen by my Father. I'd gone far outside my boundaries and found myself sitting on the rock, waiting to be noticed.

When I saw Mrs. Whyte at the bus stop, I knew that God saw me. This unexpected encounter was proof enough…at least for me. It's hard to relate for others how significant this experience was for my life. Remember, encounters with God are personal.

The first time I met Mrs. Whyte, I was a confused consultant preparing for my overseas trip. Meanwhile, something else was going on in my life. Stephanie and I had been taking steps toward working with an organization that taught biblical principles about money—helping people to achieve financial peace and freedom for their lives. As part of this journey, I was also growing enthusiasm to be a messenger for a particular biblical theme—giving!

So when I told an elderly, penniless lady to give from her meager possessions, I was essentially telling God that I would tell *anyone* about His giving truths. (Yikes!)

Following God Through Seasons of Doubt

When you begin to follow God in a new direction, moments of great assurance are followed by seasons of great doubt. You step out in faith and follow what you believe to be God's leading, then you have a crisis in faith. Later you find some much-needed confidence and respond to what feels like God's voice, then you go spiritually deaf and start doubting again.

Past encounters with God that led you to take next steps can come to feel more like coincidences. The clear conviction you had can turn to feelings of mushy doubt or fearful retreat.

Walking with God is a test of endurance for your faith. But fear and doubt are not always bad. In fact, God can use these emotions if we'll learn to use them to walk closer with Him.

You and I are not faith robots. Even Jesus was tempted to doubt (see Hebrews 4:15). God knows we sometimes need multiple encounters to stay the course He has for us. I'm convinced God moves us toward moments of weakness to keep us coming back to Him for more. More encounters, more connecting, more walking together.

Remember when Gideon asked the angel for a buzzer-shot signal to confirm that God really was speaking to him? Well, Gideon got what he asked for. He was convinced he had "seen the angel of the LORD face to face" (Judges 6:22). His confidence was at a new high. But the next day he was not so sure, so he sent out additional buzzer-shot requests to God.

When I told Mrs. Whyte to give her rice and beans, I must have been feeling really good about the giving message that day. I was bold, confident, and self-assured.

But shortly afterward, I was having doubts again. The encounter caused me to look in the mirror and ask myself: *How much do you really believe in this message, Jeff? Why did you tell her that? What business do you have talking to a needy woman about giving?*

Dear God, please get me away from this message!

My Hero Thomas

I wonder how many Christians will apologize to the disciple Thomas in heaven. He inherited a reputation as a doubter. (How would you like to have your life summarized in your weakest moments?) In my opinion, it's an identity that is way overblown. I don't want to be among those who trash his name.

Maybe it's because I am just like Thomas.

Jesus died, and He rose again. There's a two-thousand-year movement built on this premise—it's called Christianity. But before the whole world learned of this resurrection event, Jesus appeared first to just a few people. When Thomas found out from friends that they had seen Jesus, he wasn't so convinced. Thomas basically said, "Look, if you saw Jesus, that's great. But I won't believe it until I see Him with my own eyes. I want to see the scars in His hands. My faith needs that kind of proof."

If I were in Thomas's position, being told by people that they saw Jesus after He had just died, I probably would have reacted exactly the same way. Someone else's experience is not enough for me. I want my own. In fact, that is what we're talking about in *Divine Applause.* Getting your own signature moments with God, your own proof of His presence.

In the months following my initial encounter with Mrs. Whyte, I wrestled often over the meaning of our conversation. I also wondered if God was really involved in the words I had spoken. I had prayed for His assistance during that grocery store encounter. When I was in a doubting mood, I might try to push the memories out of my mind, telling myself it was just a sweet conversation with a sweet lady, but that was it.

But when she and I met the second time, on the fortieth day of my forty-day fast, I was able to view our previous encounter differently. My doubts were defeated and my faith renewed. Once again I believed God really had been with me on that winter afternoon two years prior. He had guided a hungry elderly lady into my path, and He had guided the words that I shared with her.

I found new energy in the conviction that the message of giving is really important to our walk with God. I also found my next assignment.

When Doubts Are Cleared, the Stakes Are Raised

Remember, when God gives us special encounters, they bring greater responsibilities. For Gideon this meant going into battle leading a downsized army. For Thomas this meant walking with the disciples and moving on with the Great Commission. For me, a second encounter with the rice-and-beans lady was another buzzer-shot moment that I needed as I continued down the path God had for me.

God knew I needed something undeniable, and He gave it to me. The encounter served as loud, clear marching orders: "Go do it!" And that's what I did.

Ultimately, God used this encounter and others to lead me to launch a ministry called Acceptable Gift. It's one of the few organizations that exist to teach on the sensitive subject of giving. I also wrote the book *Plastic Donuts,* based on a story about a gift from my eighteen-month-old daughter, Autumn. Today this message is being shared by churches and ministries all over the world.

This ministry may never have happened without my rice-and-beans shopping encounter, or without the follow-up encounter at the end of my forty-day fast. Another big surprise of my walk-with-God journey has been discovering a calling as a writer. (That is far from the path I started down years ago as a number-cruncher.) While this is all a part of my story, you have a unique story too. You also might be pondering some life-altering ideas as part of *your* walk with God. Perhaps you are thinking about changing careers, launching a new business, or maybe enrolling in college or seminary. Or you might be thinking of entering the mission field, planting a church, starting a nonprofit ministry or a coffee-shop Bible study.

Whatever it is that you're walking toward, as you keep walking, God gives you just what you need at the moment to fuel your faith and keep moving. There will be periods of silence, waiting, uncertainty, and even doubt. Expect those, then refuse to quit.

Eventually, another encounter with God will come along to refuel your faith and remind you of what you desperately need to know: God is watching you and affirming His plans for you.

And Now, Back to Giving

During the now-famous Secret Sermon, Jesus taught on giving, then prayer, then fasting. Then He circled back around to preach some more on giving.

In similar fashion, before we move on to the last part of *Divine Applause*, I have one more lesson on giving to share. If we understand the main point, it will help us understand all the other choices that help us walk with God.

This last giving lesson has to do with an image I couldn't quite grasp when I connected with Mrs. Whyte the second time—when she tried to answer my intruding questions about her life. It has to do with that mysterious blue chair.

14

The Power of Choices
That Please God

Several weeks after my fasting journey and my buzzer-shot encounter with Mrs. Whyte, I planned a surprise visit for her in return. I say "surprise" because I had no way to notify her, only an address.

Austin, almost an eight-year-old, would be tagging along. He was with me when the first encounter occurred, and I wanted Mrs. Whyte to see how he had grown.

As a kid, I remember making similar trips with my dad. He often reached out to people who were lonely or isolated, in need of someone to stop by for a visit and show an interest.

We all need encounters with the poor. And I'm not talking about encounters so we can solve problems, fix the system, or even "teach a man to fish." Sometimes it's more about what *we* need than about a need we're trying to meet. Interacting with the poor refines our perspective and softens our hearts.

And more importantly, encounters with the poor mean an encounter with Jesus, who assured us, "Whatever you did for one of the least of these...you did for me" (Matthew 25:40). Our gifts to the needy connect us directly to God.

On the day that Austin and I went to visit Mrs. Whyte, Stephanie prepared bags of groceries for us to bring. Austin and I drove to the outskirts of downtown, found a parking spot, and made our way toward a residential high-rise. I'd been downtown frequently but had never before noticed this building.

As we approached the main entrance, we passed smokers loitering on the sidewalks. Austin scooted closer to me, signaling his apprehension. As we walked in the front doors, we saw a small office straight ahead. The structure felt more like a municipal building than a residential one. We took a left (just a guess) and walked down the hall, trying to appear as if we knew where we were going.

Our destination was on the lower level beneath the ground floor. As we exited the elevator, I saw that Mrs. Whyte's apartment was one of the first doors down the hall. I took a deep breath, knocked…and waited. We heard a soft voice (actually, Austin did). Then the door opened, and there stood Mrs. Whyte.

Have a Seat

She seemed happy to see us. Her smile was wide and welcoming. I was no longer a nosey stranger at a bus stop; this time I was her guest.

One step past the doorway and we were in her kitchen. I handed her the bags of food and briefly listed the contents. She thanked me and sat them on bare countertops. My eyes scanned the closed kitchen cabinets, wondering what was behind the doors.

A few more steps and we were in her living room. This was also her bedroom, and her *only* room. Then straight ahead I saw it: Mrs. Whyte's chair. It was a simple, blue recliner. And it was the only piece of furniture in the apartment. The chair was a place to sit, and it was her bed too. She could recline in it at bedtime, then bring it back to the upright position in the morning.

I reflected back to our conversation weeks ago, when I was struggling to envision this apartment containing only a chair. Now I understood.

She offered us a seat. Accepting her invitation felt strange. Where would *she* sit? But it did seem like the right thing to do, so I sat in the chair and Austin sat in my lap.

Mrs. Whyte stood in front of us, at a comfortable distance but close enough so we could chat. There was no nightstand or lamp, no stack of mail...or even a newspaper. Aside from the chair, there were only two other items in the room. One was a large duffel bag pushed against the wall. That must have been her dresser for clothes, since there was no closet.

There also was an ironing board topped with an iron. That seemed odd. When I asked about it, she said she ironed clothes to earn extra money. Suddenly I felt something in my throat. (I think it was a humble pill.)

As I was recalling my earlier bus-stop instructions to give from her twenty dollars and bags of groceries, familiar thoughts were coming back to me. *I can't believe I told her that. If those are the right words for her, I wonder what they mean for me?*

During my first encounter with Mrs. Whyte nearly two years earlier, God used her to teach me about giving. This time, as I sat in her only chair assessing her meager circumstances and her income-producing ironing board, I saw that it was happening once again. I was a student sitting in my instructor's chair.

Your Chair

As we learned from John's prophetic teachings, giving is for everyone, even Mrs. Whyte. And everyone has opportunity to give and be noticed by God, no matter how limited the circumstances.

In the Old Testament, God desired that everyone—even the poor—bring burnt offerings to the festivals. There was a gift scale linked to a person's financial ability. In other words, it all depended on the particular chair that person owned.

For the poor, an acceptable animal sacrifice (remember, *acceptable* means "pleasing") could be a pigeon or a dove. Those who sat in nicer chairs, such as landowners, might give a lamb. And for those who possessed more elaborate chairs, they might bring a bull to the sacrifice. The gift standard depended on the giver's chair, his or her ability.

We don't offer burnt offerings today; still, the principle of ability-based giving applies. Paul told the Christians living in Corinth that God's measuring stick for their gifts would be based on their abilities (see 2 Corinthians 8:12).

Mrs. Whyte had one chair and no bed (or one bed and no chair, depending on how you view it). She had a tiny ability. Today, I have a house with six beds and literally dozens of places to sit. If you came to my home, you would see that I have a nice chair—especially compared to what most people in the world have. If you purchased this book at a store or downloaded it to an electronic device, you likely have a nice chair too.

Of course our abilities go beyond money and possessions. My chair includes a faith legacy, my parents, my wife and children. It includes my college education, my physical and mental abilities, and my network of friends. If you take the time to examine your chair, you'll realize just how expansive your blessings really are.

Seeking to please God through giving starts with understanding your chair. God is aware of your abilities and wants you to be aware of them too. Not everyone has the same ability. Therefore not everyone is expected to give the same gift.

The Most Popular Girl in School

Most high schools have a most popular girl. Everyone has an opinion of her, even if they don't know her well. Some of the students love her—they elevate her to homecoming queen. Others despise her—they resent all the attention she gets. Wherever she goes, people are watching.

In a financial-giving context, the most popular figure is the tithe. Everyone, whether they support or oppose this teaching, has an opinion about tithing: the practice of giving one-tenth of one's income to God's work. Emotions run high on the subject.

For some, the tithe reminds people of the good behavior they were taught to follow in Sunday school. For others, the tithe is a reminder of unattainable regulations and unanswered questions, the things they want to escape.

I've done quite a bit of thinking and study about this aspect of the Christian life. Honest study suggests there is no biblical giving measurement that applies to everyone. In fact, it's possible that your giving 10 percent, or even beyond, may not please God. It's also possible that giving less than 10 percent can be pleasing to God. This truth unsettles some people. It's supposed to.

It is true that God measures our gifts and that certain gifts sparkle more than others. We learn from Jesus's applause of the generous widow at the Temple that God measures our gifts according to how much our gift costs us. He measures it according to our unique sacrifice.

Secrets of a Troubled Tither

When I was a boy I learned to calculate 10 percent of my allowance, cash gifts, and the money I earned doing odd jobs. I tithed throughout childhood and as a teenager. I kept up this practice after college when I was working my first job. I even tithed my profits from winning the March Madness office pool one year.

I tithed because I loved God, and because it seemed like the right thing to do. And I know God honored this practice in my life. But when you practice the habit of tithing from childhood, it becomes sort of easy to do. It's like brushing your teeth at bedtime—seriously, it's possible to be completely checked out while writing checks.

Here's a confession: I especially liked tithing because of the control I felt over the remaining 90 percent. By giving God the tithe (one-tenth), the rest was for me to use to satisfy my desires. Tithing removed the need to make choices. Just give a tenth, check the box, and get back to my life.

But over time, the comfort with tithing began to give way to an inner tension—the tension between following a prescribed percentage and following my heart. I was an accountant who did my work according to established standards, and losing peace about giving a straight 10 percent troubled me.

Early in our marriage, Stephanie and I sensed God leading us to a journey in the area of financial giving. So we did what you do when you're trying to hear God. We prayed, studied the Bible, and shared our thoughts with each other. We didn't hear any voices, but we sensed God nudging us to give more. And as we surveyed our chair (our abilities), we knew we needed to take our gifts more seriously.

Over the next several years, giving considerations took center stage in our financial lives. What once was just another line item in our budget became the lens through which we viewed our overall finances. The house we lived in, the cars we drove, the idea of investing for the future—all these choices were channeled through a more important choice: how much will we give to God?

The Power of Choices

The Christian life is a journey of choices. Reading Scripture is guided by choices—which Bible translation to select, which passages to study, and how frequently to read.

Consider the practice of prayer and fasting—choices. How about determining a church home for your family and the style of preaching, teaching, and worship you prefer—choices.

Loving God and walking with Him is a choice. Giving should be guided by choices as well. When the Israelites brought gifts to the tabernacle or later to the Temple, God expected a gift from everyone. But it was up to each person to determine the amount of his or her gift (see Deuteronomy 16:16–17). Paul reminded the Christians living in Corinth to give, but the amount was for them to determine (see 2 Corinthians 9:6–7).

When we give, we are expressing our childlike and freewill choice to say, "Father God, this much is for You."

King Solomon chose to offer one thousand burnt offerings to God. Zacchaeus, a repentant tax collector, chose to give half of his possessions to the poor. When Ananias and Sapphira lied about the gifts they had brought to the apostles, Peter reminded them it had been their choice to give a gift or to give no gift at all. The property was theirs to keep and theirs to give. Lying about it was their downfall. (Literally!)

When I selected an engagement ring for Stephanie, I spent weeks examining stones, talking (sometimes haggling) with diamond merchants, and counting my nickels. I ran my calculator to determine what impact the purchase of a small, medium, or large diamond would have on our financial situation. The ring-selection process consumed my energy and my heart. It was the most exciting gift I'd ever given, and Stephanie sensed every bit of my excitement when I presented it to her.

Remember, God notices your gifts. So when you choose to buy a home and run the numbers to determine how it might affect your monthly giving budget, God notices what that decision means to you. He sees how the choices involved flow from your heart.

When you are deciding whether to buy a new car or keep driving the old one because of how it might affect your gift to the church's capital campaign, God notices the trade-offs being played out in your mind.

When you ponder selling an investment or dipping into your savings or postponing a new laptop purchase so you can support a missionary, God notices what this means for you.

Our gifts are measured by how they feel to God, which is connected to how the gift feels to us. They are not measured by how much they help others, how the gift solves a problem or meets a need, or how generous someone else considers your gift to be. If your decision to give 5 percent of your income (or 1 percent or even one dollar) causes your heart to beat faster and your hands to sweat, then that healthy tension can make your gift matter both to you and to God.

But if giving a tenth (or even a third or a half) of your income becomes a routine payment and causes your giving to be a simple decimal-point calculation, something may be missing. Remember, God enjoys your sacrifice for Him. And sacrifice only matters if it's a choice.

Giving Rules and Living Rules Are the Same

When people gain a clear, biblical understanding of how God sees giving, it also helps them understand prayer, fasting, and other expressions of walking with God. Otherwise people tend to hold two different mind-sets for walking with God: one for living and another for giving.

The three ingredients from Jesus's Secret Sermon—giving, praying, and fasting—have been created for you! Each is a gateway to connect with God. There are no biblical formulas for how much you should pray or fast or read the Bible. And there are no biblical formulas for how much you should give.

The rule for giving is the same as the rule for living: "There are no rules." There are no minimums; there are no maximums. And the degree to which we engage in these activities is determined the same way we accept salvation from God: it is our choice.

As soon as any of the secret ingredients become prescribed for you, they become less about your choices and more about measuring up. Instead of seeing God as a Father we can please, we imagine the He is holding a clipboard, checking off items listed underneath our names.

Some Can Be Pleasing

I'll never forget when I encouraged Mrs. Whyte to share some of her food and money, and that Jesus would see it and be pleased. For food she had some rice and beans and assorted other groceries; for money she had twenty dollars.

I could have told her to give away two dollars, a tenth of the twenty-dollar bill. Or maybe she could have divided her food items into ten piles and set aside one of the piles. But when it came to deciding how much to give to the God of the heavens, that was her choice to make.

I knew that whatever she gave, Jesus would see it. And while I'm in no position to judge anyone's giving, I was certain that whatever amount of money or food Mrs. Whyte might decide to give, Jesus would be pleased.

God places us on earth at different times and gives each of us unique abilities, financial and otherwise. When it comes to understanding our own abilities, sometimes we can see them more clearly while sitting in someone else's chair.

Months after my visit to Mrs. Whyte's apartment, the time I sat in her only chair, I made another trip to see her. I knocked on the apartment door, but she didn't answer. Someone else answered, and that person knew nothing about a lady named Mrs. Whyte. I knocked on other apartment doors nearby, and those who lived there did not even know who Mrs. Whyte was. She had moved, but no one could tell me where she had gone.

I never saw Mrs. Whyte again. But wherever she was, I knew God was taking care of her, just as He had the day He sent her to the little hair salon looking for rice and beans.

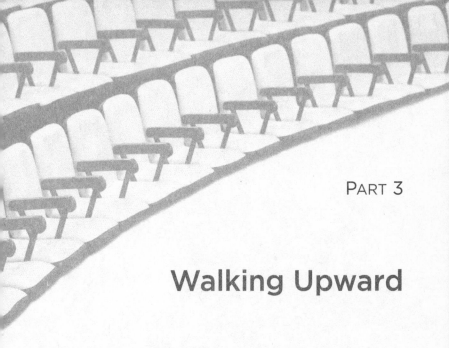

PART 3

Walking Upward

As we talk about stepping outside the norm and adopting practices that invite God's attention, we are describing a very different way to live. Jesus made this stunningly clear in Matthew chapter 6. God is looking for people who are looking for Him.

Jesus gave us three secret ingredients to help us connect with an invisible God. He taught us to do these things in secret, and He promised that we would be rewarded. Walking with God involves seeing differently (part 1) and taking some bold steps (part 2).

Seeing differently involves seeing God's delight in us, just as a loving Father hopes we will. Your Father is interested; He watches and is pleased with you. Taking bold steps involves living differently: giving in ways that get God involved, learning to hear God's voice, praying with intensity and in ways that bring out the hunger in you.

Meanwhile God is at work as well. He's helping you see your potential, charting your next steps, nudging you toward new experiences, offering reminders about tomorrow. When we live this way, the walk feels lighter. This leads to walking upward...and homeward.

15

Stars on the Ground

The secret ingredients of a walk with God can be empty unless your whole being is engaged. If you do things only out of duty or obligation or without regard for the heart, you might be wasting your time.

But the heart is a tricky thing to understand. What flows from the heart is invisible...to us. That's why, when we talk about having a good heart or loving God with all our heart, we don't always have a clear vision of what that looks like. But from God's view, it's crystal clear. He can see it like a burning sun.

Stars in the Sky

A key way God measures our hearts is by our obedience. In other words, God wants us to be blameless. I can almost see you roll your eyes, saying "Sure, Jeff. Be *blameless*. That's *all* I need to do?"

Don't close the book just yet. We're about to gain a biblical perspective on blamelessness that can change your understanding of walking with God.

God isn't surprised that we mess up or that we keep messing up, repeatedly. Still, He seeks blameless children. It sounds contradictory, I know. You might think I'm delusional or that God is seeking something that you can't possibly deliver.

Or can you? Blamelessness is a theme we see woven throughout Scripture. Ever since the disobedience of the first humans in the garden, God has sought blameless children. Noah "was a righteous man, *blameless* among the people of his time, and he walked with God" (Genesis 6:9). God told Abram to "walk before me and be *blameless*" (Genesis 17:1). Job "was *blameless* and upright; he feared God and shunned evil" (Job 1:1). Zechariah and Elizabeth "were upright in the sight of God, observing all the Lord's commandments and regulations *blamelessly*" (Luke 1:6). The apostle Peter encourages us to "make every effort to be found spotless, *blameless*" before God (2 Peter 3:14).

Blamelessness is walking with God in obedience, faithfulness, and love; it involves submitting to God and resisting evil. Blamelessness speaks to our thoughts and motives; it cuts deep into the heart and soul and goes deeper than outward actions.

And here is something that will encourage you. Your blamelessness is not determined by outside observers, even the people who know you best. It is defined and recognized only by God.

God has given us the potential to live a life that *He* considers blameless. "The LORD...delights in those whose ways are *blameless*" (Proverbs 11:20).

Paul wrote that when we are "*blameless* and pure," we "shine like stars in the universe" (Philippians 2:15).

While we look up toward the stars to see God, He is looking down to see stars on the ground.

Be All You Can Be... Why Not Blameless?

An old US Army advertising campaign used the slogan "Be all you can be." Recruiters wanted young men and women to believe in themselves and dare to achieve great things. Implied in the slogan was an equally important message: the US Army believes in you too.

We tell kids that nothing is impossible. High schools and universities pay big fees to commencement speakers to tell graduates they can become president, be a Navy SEAL, run a company, become the next Steve Jobs or Bill Gates.

But when it comes to Christian living, we repeatedly get the opposite message. We're told we are sinners. We are taught that we can't expect to live as anything other than sinners. We accept the label as easily as we accept the name we were given at birth. Being pure or holy is said to be an unreachable goal this side of heaven. Sure, it's good to try. But no one should expect much. After all, we're sinners.

It's ironic. We lie to kids and tell them they can do anything to reach their worldly dreams (not every kid can be president), but we tell Christians, who are actually new creations in God's Spirit, that they are stuck in sin and can't expect to live differently before God (arguing against something that God desires for each of us).

What did Jesus mean when He told the adulterous woman to "go, and sin no more" (John 8:11, KJV)? He must have believed in something greater for her life. And when He preached to the crowds, "Be perfect, therefore, as your heavenly Father is perfect" (Matthew 5:48), He had something greater in mind for them too.

I'm inspired by the idea that God's eyes are looking for blameless walkers. Yes, it sounds daunting. And when you think about it, that's what makes it attractive.

In addition to your having a closer, more personal walk with God, the world needs this experience too. The world is looking for people who really do live differently, not just talk differently. Sadly, many Christians don't believe a person can really be changed.

First, a Warning

If you talk to people about blameless living, things can get interesting. When you point out that God wants us to live blamelessly, they often get nervous. We are conditioned to be aware of our sin and faults. As a result, we have trouble embracing the idea that we can shine like stars to God.

A discussion about blameless living often turns to the definition of words such as *perfect, pure, holy, sinless, sanctified,* and *glorified.*

And be ready for some to pull out a list of verses reminding you of our fallen nature, our wicked ways, our deprived minds, and the reasons we can't be free from sin. (It is fun to watch left brainers and right brainers go at it.) These are all interesting topics, but they can distract us from the core issue.

So what is blamelessness really about?

For us, blamelessness is an attitude, an approach to living. It's not perfection by our own standard or anyone else's standard. It's an attitude of your heart, offered up to God.

The truth is, while we still live on earth no one is fully redeemed (a complete renewal awaits us at the resurrection). Even the stars, made by God's hands, are not completely pure in His eyes (see Job 25:5). But God is the judge of what He considers blameless, not us. And in some mysterious way, He chooses to view some of His children as these shining stars. I want to be one of them. How about you?

We All Want a Challenge

A twenty-six-year-old church leader shared some surprising thoughts with me.

My generation wants to be challenged. We want to be all or
nothing, not somewhere in the middle. We're not interested in
the stable corporate job, but we'll give our lives to Africa for an
adventure. We're not as interested in giving to a building, but
we'll give all we've got to a cause.

I've heard researchers describe Millennials in these terms. But this
man's next statement surprised me:

We're tired of being coddled with only the message of grace and
acceptance. We want something more. We want to be challenged
to fully obey God!

Has the emphasis on avoiding "blameless" talk removed adventure
and challenge from the picture? Blameless living is not just sought by
God; it is desired by Christians who are wired to want to live differently.

King David was ambitious when it came to blameless living. He knew
God had eyes scanning the universe for this kind of living. In David's mind,
God was not looking for people to mess up; instead, He was looking for
those who might step up in pursuit of pleasing Him. With this in mind,
David invited God to examine his ways and search out his heart and
thoughts. "Vindicate me, O Lord, for I have led a blameless life.... Test me,
O Lord, and try me, examine my heart and my mind" (Psalm 26:1–2).

"Look at me!" David seems to shout. Now that's bold.

Often Christians want to debate which sins, behaviors, or lifestyles
are "tolerated" by God. They toss around the "grace" card to justify their
ways. Instead of aiming to please God, they create excuses to please themselves. Don't settle for what God *might* allow. Set the bar high and ponder
what it means to be blameless before God.

There are two ways to view the pursuit of blamelessness. One comes with shackles around the feet. The other comes with hands of encouragement on the shoulder. There is a huge difference between being told you *must* be blameless and that you *can* be blameless.

Forgetful God

Early on in this book I told about the time I lost it when my sons were stomping around like elephants upstairs at home. I erupted at them. And then, to my horror, realized I had pocket-dialed my phone so that a church elder heard every word.

Fortunately I recovered rather quickly. My sons have forgiven me (and trust me, I seek their forgiveness regularly). And my friend who heard every bit of my meltdown on the phone, well, I trust he has moved past it too.

While I'm more concerned about what God thinks than what my friends think, I'm also more comforted by what God can forget.

King David, known by God as "a man after my own heart" (Acts 13:22), was comfortable living fully in God's sight. But somehow God's watchful ways slipped David's mind. David had a devastating crash. Perhaps you've read about the adultery incident with Bathsheba and David's subsequent attempt to cover it up by conspiring to have her husband killed.

They didn't have cell phones back then, but they did have roaming prophets. After his sin with Bathsheba, and then compounding the sin by having an honest man killed, David was confronted by the prophet Nathan. David finally remembered God had been watching everything.

After he received Nathan's alert, David was immediately broken… and repentant. "I have sinned against the LORD," he said.

What Nathan said next is most comforting: "The LORD has taken away your sin" (2 Samuel 12:13).

Wow! David learned a golden truth. Our sins are something God can forget. Immediately!

You and I absolutely never want to disappoint a close friend, our spouse, our kids. When mistakes are made, when selfishness rises up, blamelessness can be reset. But only if both parties are in agreement to forget.

Often in an attempt to walk with God, one party is unwilling to hit the Reset button. And it isn't God who fails to let go of the past. It's us.

Yes, shame is real. It's part of the sin package. And yes, our sins bear consequences that can last a lifetime. But God wants us to make use of His reset for our hearts, a reset that can give us instant peace. We can't experience a clean slate if we continue to replay past sins in our minds and walk with our eyes on the ground. We have to look up toward our Father.

God is not the one hitting the Rewind button.

Baby Steps

One New Year's Day I initiated a reset moment in my heart. I determined that as I began a new year I would be blameless for as long as I could. It helped that it was a holiday, a day away from work to enjoy my family and reflect on blameless walking. I would be careful to watch my words, my attitude, my tone, my thoughts…you know, the basics.

The funny thing is, while I was focused on being blameless, I seemed to notice that others weren't so blameless. In this case, members of my family!

The kids were doing their thing, arguing over week-old Christmas gifts, jockeying for time with their video games. And even Stephanie seemed irritated by my unusually smooth and controlled posture. She was much more accustomed to her husband the elephant tamer.

Somehow, even as I was surrounded by my family of sinners, I maintained a spirit of gentleness, self-control, and pure-headed thinking. (It felt as if this lasted for days. But it could have been just a few hours—or minutes!) Without realizing it, I stopped thinking about being blameless and slid back into my normal tempo, eventually barking at the stomping elephants again.

After reflecting on these moments, I wasn't sad or dejected. Jesus teaches us to clean our slate every day by seeking forgiveness (see Matthew 6:12). The same Jesus who challenges us to be perfect recognizes we need forgiveness regularly. This motivates me to start fresh each day and resume my pursuit of a blameless walk with God.

The idea of blameless living is never a burden. It's the opposite. The potential for us to be blameless frees us from shame and the burden of past mistakes. And it's equally freeing to know that when we do stumble, God is there to help us walk toward Him (see Psalm 37:24).

Perspective is critical. If you seek to delight God, the walk will feel light and freeing. But if you seek to avoid disappointing God, a blameless walk will feel heavy and burdensome. Choose the lighter load, not the heavy one. And remember, you have access to the Reset button.

Paul admitted his struggle with the urge to do things he should avoid and the failure to do what he ought to do (see Romans 7:18–19). Still, he pursued a blameless life. He told the believers in the Thessalonian church, "You are witnesses, and so is God, of how holy, righteous and *blameless* we were among you who believed" (1 Thessalonians 2:10).

Paul's words do not indicate that blamelessness is out of reach. Peter also saw the potential for holy living. "But just as he who called you is holy, so be holy in all you do; for it is written: 'Be holy, because I am holy'" (1 Peter 1:15–16).

If you can be blameless for ten seconds, why not ten minutes? And if ten minutes, why not ten hours? Blamelessness—pure, different, spotless living—is an attainable goal.

Remember we're stars, but we live on the ground. Sometimes we may feel more like blinking lights (sin, reset, sin, reset). But God knows how to read a heart that strives to be blameless and to please Him.

Walking More Closely with God

Blameless living goes hand-in-hand with walking with God. When you seek blamelessness, you are constantly thinking of God. With every decision you make, His face comes to mind.

When you're thinking of God all the time, you're thinking about how you talk to or about one another, the websites you visit, the way you complete your tax returns, the movies you watch, how you discipline your children (gulp), how closely you observe the speed limit (big gulp!).

This healthy awareness of God will translate into a desire to walk closer to Him. Jesus said, "If you love me, you will obey what I command" (John 14:15).

It's possible.

Jesus also said, "He who loves me will be loved by my Father, and I too will love him and show myself to him" (John 14:21). Did you catch that? God will show Himself to you through His applause as you aim to love Him through blameless living. Do you believe it?

As you try on this perspective, you'll notice you can pick up the pace and start walking upward.

16

Trading Up

As Stephanie and I approached our two-year wedding anniversary, we found ourselves with two solid jobs and a nine-month-old baby. Our friends were locking in mortgages, so we decided to do some house shopping.

It all seemed so stable and expected. Get married, get jobs, have a baby, buy a house. In a weird way, our predictable life together made me nervous. I recalled the advice given by so many of my senior golfing buddies years earlier: "Take risks."

So we did.

I left my secure job to become a stock day-trader. My friends thought my decision was crazy; for me, that made it more appealing. Stephanie was all for it since it meant she would give up her job, too, so we could live near family. All she asked was that I bring home the bacon for our small tribe of three.

In starting my new profession, we had to make a few trades. After trading two good jobs for no job, we traded our low-cost, employer-provided health coverage for the high-cost kind.

Next was a change in our living quarters. We left our apartment near the mountains, moved back to our home state, and put house shopping on hold. While alternating between thinking I was dumb, crazy, or brilliant, our small family moved in with my mom and dad.

Talk About Risk

The voices in one ear cheered me on, while the voices in the other told me to grow up. After all, I had responsibilities. Fortunately, my wife numbered among the cheerleaders. As for bringing home the bacon, we ate from my parents' fridge for a while.

And the perks? I traded dark suits and ties for shorts and sandals. Instead of tracking a time sheet, recording what was accomplished every fifteen minutes, I began tracking red-and-green ticker symbols.

Each day I strolled into the trading room, a dimly lit office where I rented a computer terminal for stock trading. Lining the walls were others who, like me, most likely had left behind a life that seemed far more secure. My new colleagues included retired folks, young guns like myself, and others representing all stages of life in between.

Emotions ran high. Some traders reacted to disappointment by smashing keyboards, throwing things, and screaming choice words about someone on the other side of the trade; others were silent and nearly immobile.

One afternoon, during my first month of trading, Stephanie came to the office to watch me work. It would be her last trip to the trading room…ever. (Something about a weak stomach.)

For several weeks I lost money almost every day. Our savings were disappearing faster than a box of donuts left in the break room. I desperately wanted to be a trader. I also wanted to remain a husband and a father. And both of us wanted to move out of my parents' basement.

The risk-taking voices in my head praised my efforts. But I realized I never had asked my seasoned golfing buddies what to do when risk taking didn't pan out. Why did they never tell me *those* stories?

Thankfully, I was able to master a trading pattern called a "breakout," and that's what turned things around. A breakout is when the value of a stock (or anything tradable: commodities, metals, currencies) suddenly breaks out into a higher, unfamiliar trading territory. When that happens, look out!

A Crash Course

Let's imagine you're a trader of pork bellies.

Futures contracts on these twenty-ton containers of meat are no longer traded as they were decades ago. But I love bacon, so let's pretend it's tradable again. But instead of having to buy truckloads of uncooked pork, you can buy shares of stock in a pork-belly company that sells pork to customers, by the ice-chest full, to take home to the family. (This is a bacon-eater's dream.)

Suppose these pork belly shares are trading between forty-eight and fifty dollars on Monday. Buyers and sellers are comfortable with the prices in this range.

The market is active, and when the price hits fifty dollars, sellers are happy to sell. As they do, the selling pressure pushes the price back down toward forty-eight dollars. At that level, buyers become hungry for deals and start buying more stock. That pushes the price back up toward fifty dollars.

This goes on for a while (days, weeks, or even months). Buyers like to pick up this stock at forty-eight dollars, and sellers like to unload it at fifty dollars. Traders call this "trading in the channel." Over time, a sideways-moving trading pattern develops where the price stays confined to this tight price range. (See chart on page 167.)

But eventually either buyers or sellers will take over and move the price outside the range.

Suppose, due to their health-giving properties (pork is gluten free, right?), Bacon-O's become hugely popular for breakfast. Interest in pork bellies grows, and investors who hold pork belly shares are less likely to sell at fifty dollars. Sellers hold onto their pork-belly equity. Eventually, hungry buyers will push the price to fifty-one dollars, fifty-two, and beyond.

POP!

You know that sensation when you open a bottle of soda pop and all the pent-up energy is released? That's similar to what happens with a stock breakout. The buildup of buying energy creates pressure at the top. When the cap is removed, it pops!

With true breakouts, the price shoots up like a rocket. Using our pork-belly example, prices would reach fifty-four, fifty-five, or even sixty dollars. It might be pork bellies or shelled corn or shares in an Internet start-up that's showing promise. Traders all over the world are watching for game-changing encounters. When a breakout occurs, the trading room goes crazy and everyone pounds on their keyboards trying to get in on the action.

Left-behind traders often smack their computer monitors in frustration and blame it on the software or some unknown broker in New York. It's a lot like a major league outfielder missing a pop fly, then glaring at his glove.

For those participating in the breakout, there is profit—sometimes big profits. Traders take their money and pay their bills and buy bacon for their families.

Those who are really good at reading breakouts buy swimming pools or new cars or take their families on expensive vacations. Their lives become different.

Perhaps the most exciting aspect is this: breakouts trigger further breakouts. Stocks that trend upward over a lifetime get that way by experiencing breakout after breakout after breakout.

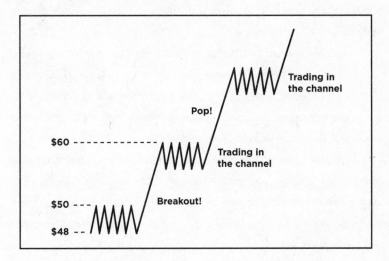

Faith Breakouts

I enjoyed an exhilarating trading career for several years. Sometimes I was able to put bacon on the table, other times it was the more economical rice and beans. But I have great memories of my years as a trader, and I have those breakout moments to thank.

While I was making a living from stock-market breakouts, it occurred to me how the profitable trade patterns look a lot like the Christian journey. Walking with God consists of faith breakouts. Opportunities, risks, and choices come together in moments of connection.

While trading in the channel of life, Christians are building a base for their faith. We seek opportunities to connect with an invisible God; we learn to build up secrets with God by praying, fasting, and meditating on His Word. We seek to live blamelessly, to give generously, and to pray with more expectancy.

Along the way, we look, listen, and expect experiences with God to bring us even closer to Him. And with these experiences come breakouts in our faith.

When a shepherd boy named David relieved a gargantuan soldier named Goliath of his hail-damaged head, that was a breakout moment. David became known as the giant-killer. Like traders sizing up a breakout stock, everyone now saw David differently. King Saul did, his brothers did, and God saw David differently too.

As people expected greater things from him, David expected greater things from himself. And like a breakout stock that keeps going up, David's breakout experience paved the way for future faith breakouts. Eventually, his walk with God brought him to the responsibility of a crown and the royal palace.

But remember, before the cage match with Goliath, David was a lion killer and a bear killer. He probably started by swatting flies and slinging stones at ravens, then moved up to coyotes. Each new breakout fed off the new courage and faith earned from a prior breakout experience.

As in the trading universe, spiritual breakouts require two ingredients for growth: base building and taking chances. In between the breakout moments, David was building a foundation for his faith: walking with God and believing that God was paying attention.

The faith of his boyhood was the foundation for his future. On that foundation he started building the godly courage needed to take more and greater risks. When the risk opportunities came, David was ready.

Remember Steve, Abraham's chief of staff? His buzzer-shot discovery of a wife for Isaac was an amazing breakout. As with David's breakout, we suspect this came on the heels of a steady, hungry walk with God, one that likely spanned decades.

This is the pattern we see with men and women who want more of God's attention, believing that they will be noticed by their Father: steady, plodding faith (walking with God in the channel), followed by life-altering encounters with God (faith breakouts).

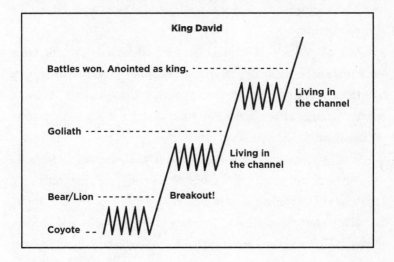

Blue-Chip Dad

When I was a toddler, something triggered a breakout in my dad's heart. He suddenly felt a desire to get his family in church.

Dad had attended church as a youth but had drifted away from the faith walk during college and his army days. As a young married man with a new baby (me), he took first steps back toward God. You could say that his decision to get his family ready to attend church was a breakout moment. On a Sunday morning he was taking a chance, acting out of character, and altering the family routine.

Soon Dad started reading the Bible. This led to his spending more time with God. He was praying, journaling, reading books, and gaining knowledge. Dad was building a base for his faith.

Along the way, he experienced moments with God, little breakouts that propelled his faith forward, giving him confidence for the next step. Sometimes the breakouts were private moments—maybe a revelation in God's Word, igniting his passion for more. Other times they were public rewards—the invitation to teach Sunday school or to serve among the church leadership.

As his experience grew, his hunger for God did too. Like a breakout stock that people notice differently, Dad began to be noticed differently. The deacons asked him to be their chairman. Churches invited him to speak. Even the poor on downtown streets noticed my dad—because he noticed them.

In between spiritual breakouts, Dad was building a base for his faith: waking up early to pray, reading God's Word, fasting, serving, and giving to others. He sought blameless living too.

Like a blue-chip stock that is trading in the channel, the changes in my dad's life were an experience of faith breakout after breakout after breakout. He was living the life of a man seeking God. And it started with taking a simple risk: he took his family to church.

Chart Scanning from Heaven

For the eyes of the LORD range throughout the earth to strengthen those whose hearts are fully committed to him. (2 Chronicles 16:9)

God is looking for faith walkers who are looking for breakouts. Are you seeking breakout encounters with God? Are you building a foundation for your faith so that you won't miss opportunities for growth?

Breakouts often come when hungry children go chasing them.

- Jesus told Peter to leave the boat for the open water, but first Peter asked Jesus to invite him to take the risk.
- Jesus had a one-on-one with Nicodemus, but it was Nicodemus who already had taken a risk in looking for Jesus during the night.
- Jesus called Zacchaeus to come down from the tree, but it was the curious tax collector who first climbed the tree to get a closer look at the Man everybody was talking about.
- Jesus healed a centurion's servant, but it was the centurion who chased Jesus down, asking for help.
- God delivered the buzzer-shot answer for Steve, Abraham's chief servant, but it was Steve who first called out to God.

You and I are a lot like Steve, Nicodemus, Peter, and the rest. We want God to show up, and God is noticing our hearts' desire to be seen by Him.

A Wild Risk to Get God's Attention

Drew was a college student who took on a summer job selling books. He was hungry to make money to pay for college. He also was hungry for God. He made a vow that whatever commission he earned, he would give half to God. Drew grew up being taught to give 10 percent of his income to his church. The idea of giving so much more was new to him. You could say this was a wild idea, a risk to get God's attention.

By summer's end, Drew's sales were off the charts. Of roughly thirty-five hundred sales producers across the country, he was the top salesperson—the absolute champion! He received a very nice payday. And he wrote a check to his church for half the amount.

It was a significant breakout experience, bolstering his faith and setting a firm foundation for God to do even bigger things over the next few decades. Today Drew owns a multistate company that employs hundreds of people. His company operates according to Christian values and everyone knows their boss worships God.

Growing Older and Wishing for More

My friend Isaac was approaching his twenty-fifth birthday and sensing an unusual hunger for more in his life with God. He committed to fasting from food for twenty-five days. Like a young child exploring a new hiking trail, Isaac set out on a brand-new journey. He had fasted only once before, and then for just one day. This was a big step.

Each night Isaac took a thirty-minute walk to talk to a God he could not see. His fasting journey was much like mine. Lots of silence and wondering if God was noticing. Along the way Isaac received fresh insights from Scripture, and he experienced a secret *whisper moment* from God. A breakout experience that still encourages him today.

My favorite part of Isaac's story is not the twenty-five-day fast, but what happened during his previous single-day fasting experience. The first day Isaac had ever fasted, he was driving a church van to a restaurant to meet friends. While circling the parking lot, he drove the van into the drive-through awning, causing significant damage. Isaac received an earful from the restaurant manager. Discouraged, Isaac went home and ate a large bag of potato chips.

It's okay to laugh at the story (I did). And I suspect God was smiling too. Sometimes our breakout efforts may seem like failures. But it's possible that Isaac's twenty-five-day fast may never have happened if not for his one-day fast attempt, which was interrupted by a bag of chips.

Remember, what may feel like an air-ball attempt to connect with God might be the very step toward a breakout in your faith.

Jabez Wanted More

We don't know much about Jabez, but we know a lot about his simple prayer, thanks in part to a highly successful little book. I like the story, and it doesn't bother me that the main character's bio is only seven words long.

"Jabez was more honorable than his brothers" (1 Chronicles 4:9).

This kind of honor is earned over a lifetime of walking with God, living in the channel. We don't have the chart of his full breakout journey, but I'm sure he had one. You don't get the distinction of being "more honorable" by just coasting along.

Then he prayed a breakout prayer: "More!"

It reads like this: "Jabez cried out to the God of Israel, 'Oh, that you would bless me and enlarge my territory! Let your hand be with me, and keep me from harm so that I will be free from pain'" (1 Chronicles 4:10).

We'd like to know more, but God does not owe us a full transcript of this guy's life. The biblical pattern shows that people who are bold and ask God for something significant also walk a pretty consistent path of humility and obedience.

What we know for sure is that Jabez stepped up with a big prayer, and my guess is that it came on the heels of earlier breakout experiences. Jabez wanted a breakout, and he got it! Verse 10 says pretty simply: "And God granted his request."

When Trading Up Means Stepping Down

Life consists of peaks and valleys. And sometimes the greatest breakouts come on the heels of our greatest trials or seasons when God remains silent.

Before Joseph was elevated to a position of ruler of Egypt, he spent years in prison. Job's family and wealth were reestablished after Job had lost everything. The Israelites' faith was bolstered when God parted the Red Sea, but only after they had endured decades of slavery. Mary gave birth to the Messiah in a manger, but only after she carried the child for nine months while dealing with strange looks from others.

Faith breakouts often are born from life's lows. It's during these darker moments when God is most invisible and silent. These moments also are when our faith speaks loudest from God's perspective. When we continue to pursue blameless living and seek out God's voice—even when we're not hearing from God or seeing Him work—God notices.

Business letdown, marriage failure, a wayward child, the death of a loved one, depression. These are times when God can seem most distant. But often what God is doing behind the scenes is allowing your perseverance to grow, and then, *pop!* You'll have your breakout moment.

Often trading up feels like trading down. But for those who love and seek God, we're promised that all things work together for good (see Romans 8:28).

Ordinary Moments

When I was sitting in the bleachers at a youth basketball game talking to God, I *saw* His attention. I know, because I saw it shining down on my son. That was a breakout. My faith shot up. I beamed with pride in my son and was humbled with awe before my Father. But this experience with God was not an isolated event. It was a part of a journey I've shared with God for many years.

Throughout my adult life I have been building on a faith foundation, aspiring to do the things Jesus teaches us to do. As I have invested in secrets and pursued blamelessness, I keep looking up along the way. These are the ordinary moments, "living in the channel."

Over time, the ordinary moments result in a surprise reward, a breakout, or a new encounter with God.

If we want to explore new walking trails with God, which bring new experiences and opportunities to grow, we all start where we are. We take steps, we take risks, and we ask for more.

What are you asking for?

17

Roosters and Wimps

As a child, I was a Rooster. My parents signed me up for soccer, and along with other kids in kindergarten I joined the Roosters. The team was named after an Australian rugby powerhouse.

Coach Nat had arrived in the States from the outback, and he brought his Aussie accent with him. My teammates and I knew nothing about soccer, and we knew even less about the Roosters from Australia. They must have been scrappy, because we little Roosters sure were. After the first year, Coach Nat moved on, then my dad coached us for the next five years.

Our name certainly helped our brand. While there were plenty of Wildcats, Roughers, Cyclones, and Cosmos, there was only one team called the Roosters.

A patch sewn onto our shirts, featuring a bright red bird, was our signature team logo. And our red, white, and blue uniforms were on the cutting edge of sports design. The gear was great, but our play was even better. The Roosters almost always went undefeated in league play and made deep runs in the postseason playoffs. We loved our mascot and the swagger that came with our victories.

One year a parent brought a caged rooster to a Saturday morning game. This creature did not resemble the smiley rooster in the cartoons. We learned that these birds are fearless protectors and watchfully aggressive.

The other team complained about the rooster, saying he was too loud, so the referee made us take him to the car. I don't know if the bird was really the problem. Maybe it was our intimidating pregame warmup that annoyed them. With our knees fully bent and crouching low to the ground, we would squat on the field, flap our arms, and crow like a flock of mad birds.

Dad never played soccer himself, but he figured out the basics and had a strong group of mini-athletes to work with. He yelled only when he was happy, and that was a lot. Rooster play was exciting. The parents especially loved watching Dad on the sidelines, jumping in the air and throwing his clipboard when we scored. Of course this got the other parents excited.

But at one of our practices, Dad was not so happy. All the players were horsing around—throwing dirt and rocks across the field, giving each other wedgies, and making noises with their hands in their armpits.

As the nonsense escalated a few more levels, Dad blew his whistle and yelled in a firm voice, "The next one who throws a rock..." Before he could complete the threat, a rock struck Dad's head. You could have heard a pin drop in the grass.

Everyone was stunned...and terrified. I'm pretty sure the rock thrower wet his pants. The other boys had not seen Dad this serious before and didn't know what might be coming next. Somehow Dad kept his cool, then huddled up his little Roosters and went on to have a more serious soccer practice.

Years later at my wedding, one of my rock-throwing friends recalled that famous event. What he remembered most was that when Dad got hit, he knew who had thrown the rock, but Dad did not single out the culprit. Instead, he calmly reprimanded the entire team. Dad was not the kind to call out another parent's kid.

Different Rules

When it came to Dad's own kid, though, different rules applied. One Saturday morning the Roosters lined up against a team that had a player who could launch the ball off his foot like a rocket. (I remember seeing smoke coming from his cleats.)

Whenever the ball entered his domain, this enemy controlled it in a slow, steady bounce, a foot or two off the ground. This was a signal; he was getting ready to wind up his leg and blast the ball to the other end of the field. My job was to block the ball.

I improvised a routine for this situation. I would run toward him, jump in the air, and turn my body one hundred eighty degrees to block the ball with my backside. I was accomplished at this maneuver and proud of being so brave. If I timed it just right, the ball would ricochet off my back and spray out of bounds or bounce off in another direction.

But my clipboard-throwing dad was not impressed. After I repeated this maneuver two or three times, I heard a screeching command from the sidelines. "Ruuuun through the baaalll. Charrrrge the baaalll!"

Then he added a statement that I will never forget. "You're not a ballerina. Stop playing like a *wimp*!"

The message was clear. Roosters do not protect themselves by deflecting a ball off their backside. Roosters charge the ball, taking a kick or deflecting the ball off the gut—or worse.

Still, my blood boiled. I resented the "wimp" label.

I did go on to play a more reckless game of soccer, and I didn't do any more ballerina spins.

In my uniform I looked like a Rooster. At practices and in pregame warmups, I was a Rooster, no question. But when it came to blocking a kick from the kid with a cannon for a leg, my play was not fitting for a Rooster. I played like a wimp.

Wimps

When it comes to Christian living, many of us are wimps. But in other areas of life we may display unexpected bravery, taking great risks to accomplish "impressive" things. I have seen Christian men and women launch or buy businesses, sell them for great gains, and pocket gobs of cash. But when it comes to worshiping God with their financial assets, they give like wimps.

Some Christians accumulate distinguished credentials and are recognized leaders in their career fields, but they rarely read the Bible. Others become teachers at universities, consultants to Fortune 500 companies, or managers to dozens of subordinates. But they can't name a single person they have discipled in the faith.

On weekends some Christians wake up early to play golf, head to the lake, hit the jogging trails, or maybe put in a few hours at the office. But the thought of waking up early to pray never enters their minds.

Just as I did the morning before a Roosters' game, they wake up on Sunday morning, put on their suits (or shorts and flip-flops), and head to church. But the rest of the week they act like ballerinas.

They don't press in for a closer walk with God. They don't really believe Jesus's sermon about pursuing God in secret and receiving rewards. They like God well enough, but they are afraid to risk loving Him.

God is looking for Roosters. Strong. Committed. Risk-taking Roosters who are hungry for rewards.

There are some rough characters in the Old Testament, God followers who did gruesome and gutsy stuff. Their weekend activities were quite different from ours. Consider Samson, who gathered three hundred foxes and tied their tails together for fun. Not your normal weekend hobby.

David's mighty men had a reputation too. One man chased a lion into a pit on a snowy day and killed it with his hands. Another killed eight hundred men with his spear while his buddy fought all day with his hand frozen to his sword. These men were wild (see 2 Samuel 23:8–23). When I see an NFL player on the sidelines, keeping warm in front of space heater while a trainer massages his ankle, I chuckle at the contrast (while I'm indoors at home, sitting in my comfy chair).

One time when King David was thirsty, his "mighty three" warriors broke through enemy ranks just to fetch him some water. These characters from the Bible are extreme risk takers. They are Roosters!

But David was a Rooster of a different class. He was humbled by the reckless devotion of the men who brought him a drink. He refused to drink the water, pouring it out instead as an offering to God. Mega-Rooster!

Roosters sacrifice their comfort, and sometimes even their lives, for something that is exceedingly greater than themselves.

Mighty You

We have mighty men and women today. They just look different.

My friend Daniel was an attorney on track to be made partner in a large law firm. The promotion would bring a significant financial reward. As a husband with three young children, he also knew it would cost him in many ways. As he surveyed the lifestyles of the other partners, he determined it wasn't worth the required time investment.

He told the partners he wasn't interested. Not only that, he also requested a three-day workweek so he could scale back his hours. He wanted to spend the other two days volunteering with his church and getting more involved in other ministries.

He was a rising star and was valued by his law firm, so his proposal was accepted. It cost him a partnership and meant a substantial cut in pay. But to him it was worth it. He is a Rooster.

I met a man who partnered with his brother to take over a small business. They decided to accept a modest salary and give all the company's profits to Kingdom work. Today the company is worth hundreds of millions of dollars, and they give millions away each year.

Every Tuesday afternoon for more than ten years, Kacie and three friends have met for prayer. Their meetings last three hours. They spend one hour in prayer and two hours in encouragement from God's Word. There is no telling how many lives have been touched by God's attention on these prayers.

Twenty-eight-year-old Tim was having dinner with friends when he suggested they all complete a forty-day fast. It was an outrageous idea, but a half-dozen unmarried men and women embraced the challenge. Among the desires they prayed for throughout the forty days was that God would bring the right spouses into their lives. Liz was among these hungry disciples. Tim and Liz were only acquaintances when the journey began. One year later I attended their wedding. (How's that for a buzzer shot?)

There are lots of Roosters out there.

Clipboard Prophets

My dad was not a hotheaded coach. After all, it was only soccer, and we were just kids.

But when it comes to Kingdom living, sometimes God's kids need the help of a hotheaded Rooster coach. Back in the day, God used prophets to call out the Israelites on their wimpy behavior. On one occasion, the Israelites were absorbed in their homes—spending large amounts of time and money building backyard fireplaces, upgrading kitchens, installing swimming pools, and replacing big barns with huge barns.

There is nothing necessarily wrong with that sort of thing, except that these do-it-for-yourselfers looked the other way as they passed the run-down Temple on their trips to Domestic Depot. Then God commissioned Coach Haggai, a prophet with both a clipboard and a temper, to set them straight.

"Is it a time for you yourselves to be living in your paneled houses, while this house remains a ruin?" (Haggai 1:4). God was talking about His house, the Temple. He wanted the people to stop being wimps and look the situation in the eye.

"Give careful thought to your ways," the prophet continued. "Go up into the mountains and bring down timber and build the house, so that I may take pleasure in it and be honored" (Haggai 1:7–8).

Did you get that? The theme of pleasing God surfaces yet again. God wants to delight in what His children do. I'm sure He likes cedar wood, but He loves it when we lock in on Him.

Apparently they listened to Haggai, the brave Rooster. "The people obeyed the voice of the Lord" and began working on God's house (Haggai 1:12, 14).

God gave a clipboard to another prophet, Malachi, whose target was a bit more focused. Malachi went after the priests, the religious leaders who had grown sloppy and even deceitful in their worship. Instead of sacrificing the best animals to God, they were setting them aside for themselves. Then they'd bring blind, lame, and crooked-legged animals to God.

God was not happy. "I will accept no offering from your hands" (Malachi 1:10). Wimpy behavior can be detestable to God. If you're a ministry leader, don't let your leadership stoop to this level.

Wimp Training

People want adventure. Whether it's skydiving, rock climbing, marathon running, or another extreme activity that stretches us, we cannot avoid the desire for challenge and significance. Likewise, Christians desire meaningful experiences in their journey with God.

But sometimes, without meaning to, leaders teach Christians to settle for small goals. I have felt this way in financial stewardship classes before. If you earn a dollar, put your dime aside for God. Really? This is not Rooster giving, at least it's not for many of North American wage earners. It's a limiting mind-set.

During the Lenten season, the forty day lead-up to Easter, churches often encourage people to give up something in their diet—some form of fast. It's true there are no rules with fasting. But this is also an area where many of us can step up.

So you want to eliminate chocolate for forty days? Or caffeine? Or your favorite dessert?

Hear me clearly; this can be a powerful experience. Truly. But consider if perhaps God is calling you for something different. If each day at work you sip on a biggie drink and take an afternoon trip to the snack machine, you might want to think of something different than forty days without chocolate cake. You're capable of a greater sacrifice. Think Rooster!

One year a Rooster leader shared that he planned to read the Bible twice, all the way through, in a year. I really wanted to do that too, but I had never even read through the Bible once. (I had tried multiple times before but usually veered off course in February or March—or the first week of January!) Still, I embraced the challenge. And because it was a more meaningful one, I altered my routine. For a year I read the Bible whenever I had a free moment. I carried a Bible to dentist appointments and took it with me in the car to the kids' activities. This also meant less time for watching television, surfing the Internet, and reading books.

That year I experienced breakouts in my faith. It was because I had embraced a Rooster assignment. People are looking for challenge. They gravitate toward bigger goals, not wimpy ones.

As a reminder, this is not about working off a task list to be a "better" Christian. It's about taking steps to encounter God and experience His applause.

If Everyone Would Blah-Blah-Blah...

Another thing that can hold us back is averaging out the expectations. You know what I mean: "If *everyone* in the church tithed, the church could quadruple the budget, pay off the mortgage, and double the missions fund." Or "If *everyone* would volunteer an hour at the food bank…" You get the idea.

I'm all for rallying the troops. Church leadership should aim to engage everyone with the mission. But sometimes, aiming for full participation only holds back the Roosters. While we're trying to get everyone with a pulse to take a small step, would-be Roosters are taking a rest. They haven't been issued a big enough challenge, so they sit this one out.

Not everyone is going to do his or her part. The Great Commission has always largely been carried on the shoulders of a few Roosters. Jesus was aware of this, and His approach to ministry showed it. He wasn't concerned about mobilizing crowds. Instead, He often escaped crowds so He could spend time with a few Roosters.

If you're a church leader, it's all right to have programs and steps for the masses. But what are you doing to uncage the Roosters?

Wake-Up Calls

As His hours on the cross drew near, Jesus wanted to prepare Peter for the massive leadership expedition to follow. Peter's readiness was not evident at first. He fell asleep in the Garden of Gethsemane, after Jesus had asked him and others to pray with Him. Shortly after that, after Jesus had been arrested and taken from the garden, Peter denied Jesus three times, just as predicted.

How fitting it was for God to commission an actual rooster to call Peter out. The rooster's crow was a wake-up call for Peter to set aside his wimpy living.

I imagine Peter reflected on all the secrets Jesus had entrusted to him. He must have realized Jesus had big plans for him, and that he wasn't up to the task. Then, through a personal encounter with Jesus in the days following the Resurrection, Peter reconnected and went on to show God's transformational strength, alongside Paul and others.

A potentially devastating moment (publically denying Jesus) would be used to set up a breakout in Peter's walk. God is masterful at using our failures to take us further.

God has a history of singling out people for fearless living. He may be calling you out. If so, it's because He loves you and wants something better for your life. Consider such a call out to be a privilege. You have God's attention.

When he coached the Roosters, my dad chose not to call out my teammates, because they didn't have the connection to him that I did. But when I kept turning my back to the hard kicks of the other team's star player, I got a direct message. After all, I was his son!

Dad's call out was a privilege. It ruffled my feathers and brought out the better in me. And after he and I went out for pizza that night, the *"ballerina"* and *"wimp"* admonitions lost their sting.

Unknowns

Before all these Bible stories were stories, they were the day-to-day lives of real people. Filled with moments of adrenaline and decision, nervousness and aliveness!

I don't know about you, but I don't enjoy watching a movie twice. Since I already know how the drama unfolds, it doesn't hold my interest the second time. This may be the same problem we have with Bible stories. We already know the ending.

When we reread the story of David the shepherd boy trying on King Saul's armor, we already know he will set it aside and battle a giant with only his sling and five stones. But we forget that when he was being urged to put on the king's armor, David did not know if he'd survive the next hour. He knew he might well be the next casualty of war.

When I read about Peter's denial of Jesus, I know already how the story ends. We know he went on to be a Rooster in God's kingdom, but in Peter's mind he was an abject failure, a chicken at a time a Rooster was needed. Peter's world went dark when the rooster crowed, fulfilling Jesus's troubling prophecy. Can you imagine?

Living as a Rooster is risky. We subconsciously expect that God will show us our happy ending before we even take the first move. So we wait. We live small. We lead small by expecting small things from others—and from ourselves.

But bold living is what gives God pleasure. And it's what gets His attention.

Not Alone

Sometimes our Rooster pursuits are silent and private endeavors. Just God and you. This is where secrets are born. But we must be careful not to take a Lone Ranger approach. We all need some company, and we need the company of Roosters, not wimps.

Back when my soccer team learned the noisy rooster strut, I thought it was pretty corny. No one was interested in doing the rooster strut alone. But when we were together on the field, we all joined in as a team and gladly did the noisy strut. Some things are easier when done with the encouragement of others.

David had Jonathan. Elisha had Elijah. The disciples had one another. When my young friends took on a forty-day fast, they had the support of one another. The power of accountability works; we all need the help of others.

As I survey the faith breakouts in my life, many were accompanied or sparked by the encouragement of a Rooster. And I've had the privilege of encouraging other Roosters. Coaches and mentors can call you out when necessary, just as my dad called me out. And they will encourage you, just as Jesus encouraged Peter. Jesus knew what was really inside of Peter: a Rooster.

You're Better

A friend of mine once shared a life-shaping experience he had nearly twenty years earlier, when he was in high school. He was a good kid, attended church, stayed out of trouble. But in a weak moment during his senior year, he was caught off guard. He and some baseball teammates thought it would be fun to try smoking pot. His dad found out, then confronted him with five words my friend has never forgotten. "Son, you're better than that."

That was it. No grounding for life. No taking away the car. Just five words. And those words spoke volumes.

My friend heard his dad saying, "Son, that's not who we are. That kind of behavior is so far outside our family values that I don't even know how to respond. But you know what? I believe in you. And you're better than that."

The father never brought it up again. A powerful call-out message shaped my friend for life—inspiring him to be a Rooster.

Maybe your sins are standing in the way of blameless living. Perhaps you've felt the sound of those very words but didn't recognize where, or Who, they were coming from.

When Nathan confronted David with his sin, part of God's message was essentially "You're better than that."

When Jesus met the woman at the well, who had a pattern of moving from one man to the next, His words to her spoke "You're better than that."

The prodigal son walked back to his father, who embraced him, kissed him, and prepared a feast. I don't know for sure, but I'm confident the boy heard something like, "Son, I knew you were better than that. Now let's eat."

Do Less, Be a Rooster

I love stories about Peter the disciple. He reminds me of, well...all of us. Like me, Peter struggled with the tension of being busy versus being with Jesus. Yes, being with Jesus involves initiative and action. But sometimes we choose the less-important activities.

When Jesus was being arrested, Peter whacked at the enemy's ear with a sword and was quickly told to put the weapon away. As Jesus picked the soldier's bloodied ear off the ground and put it back in place, I imagine Peter thinking, *I wish I'd prayed with Him earlier up on the hill.*

Remember when Peter returned from the secret walk up the mountain with Jesus, James, and John? Peter wanted to launch a project to build gazebos for Jesus, Moses, and Elijah. About that time God's voice boomed from the clouds and spooked the disciples. God wanted them to pay attention to what was happening in the moment, not plan a to-do list.

Being a Rooster is not about conquering the world and taking charge. Yes, leadership duties and busywork are part of the Christian life. But more important than our to-do list is Jesus's desire that we connect with Him. To love Him.

He'll do more through us than we can do for Him. Being a Rooster is not intended to be an exhausting experience. In fact, it might be about slowing down and taking a rest.

As the prophet Haggai wrote, "Give careful thought to your ways" (1:7). Is your life too busy? Is your family schedule maxed out? Have you constructed an impossible to-do list? It takes a Rooster to say no to the world's offerings and settle down. It's too easy to stay busy. Wimps can do that, and the Pharisees sure tried hard. Besides, there's no reward in that kind of effort.

Every morning the Rooster crows, but only after a good night's rest.

Go out there and be a Rooster!

18

Rewards at Family Camp

Gunnar was not quite four years old when we spilled the beans about our summer vacation plans. We were going back to family camp!

He remembered the previous year's trip: our whole family sleeping in a single-room cabin. He also recalled the endless chants, goofy skits, and clap-clap songs during meals. Then there was rodeo night, carnival night, face painting, and ice cream parties at the swimming pool.

I should have waited before telling the boys about our plans, but I mentioned it a few months before departure. My other two sons, Austin and Cade, were excited for a few hours, but their focus quickly returned to other things. Not so with Gunnar. He could not stop talking about family camp.

Every day he carried around the miniature photo album from the previous year's trip. And every day he asked if we were going to family camp "today." My answer, "We're going in a few months," held little meaning. He didn't understand the difference between tomorrow, next week, or next month.

Finally I said in a firm voice, "Gunnar, stop talking about family camp! We are not going there for a long, long time."

He stopped talking about family camp, and he stopped looking forward to the day. I had snuffed out my child's vision for this important experience.

When Vision Is Snuffed Out

In a similar way, Christians have been robbed of a vision for heaven. We lose sight of the reality that earth is not our home and that one day Jesus will return to gather each of God's children to our eternal home. It takes real faith to keep this scene front and center before us.

"You ought to live holy and godly lives as you look forward to the day of God and speed its coming" (2 Peter 3:11–12). Living without this vision is costly. Instead of eagerly anticipating the coming of "the Day," we settle for wimpy hopes such as going on vacation or finding a better job. There's nothing wrong with these goals, but when they crowd eternity from our imagination, our walk with God slows down...or for some, stops completely.

I suspect one cause of our disconnect is that deep down many of us don't look forward to the time when we will actually see God face to face. Because we wrongly imagine a scowl or a vacant stare on the face of God, we settle for a dim vision of heaven too.

Another obstacle is that God's home in heaven is invisible to us. Just as it's difficult to walk with an invisible God, it's hard to live with excitement for an invisible place. That is why, instead of living for faith breakouts, we allow spiritual letdowns to become the norm. And instead of aiming for buzzer shots, we don't even take a shot. Instead of creating secrets with God, we post our momentary thrills to the world on Facebook.

Without a vision for heaven we accept ordinary living. Instead of looking forward to "the Day of God," we are consumed by the day-to-day of the here and now.

But looking forward to our ultimate family camp not only improves life today, it also changes how we live every day. To live differently and walk with our invisible God, we can't allow our vision of heaven to be extinguished.

Looking Forward to What Lies Ahead

We all know what it's like to anticipate what lies ahead. It might be a ball game or concert, a birthday celebration, maybe college graduation, or a wedding.

I can get ridiculously energized by an upcoming college football game but find that I devote very little thought to heaven. How does this happen? After all, I love God and want to please Him. I want my life to count. I desire personal connections and a rich relationship with God. So why can I be so dismissive of heaven but become electrified by something as trivial as a Bowl game on television?

Again, a key challenge is that I can see things on earth, but I can't see heaven or the future rewards Jesus talked about. And this is precisely why our faith pleases God. When we long for something that we can't see (heavenly things) more than what we can see (earthly things), our faith muscles are being flexed and God is pleased.

This tension between the seen and the unseen is real. Jesus knew all about it. When He fasted for unseen things, Satan tempted Him with the seen: bread to eat and an earthly kingdom to rule. That's why Jesus was so persistent in talking about heaven.

Heavenly Minded Master

Matthew seemed particularly interested in Jesus's focus on heaven. His gospel account is saturated with sound bites of his Teacher speaking of the coming Kingdom.

If you're looking for a place to launch a new Bible-reading plan, the gospel of Matthew is not a bad place to start. The word *heaven* occurs roughly one hundred fifty times in the four Gospels, but more than half of those mentions—eighty-five—are found in Matthew.

Jesus references heaven nearly twenty times in the Sermon on the Mount (see Matthew 5–7). His Secret Sermon is right in the middle of all this heaven talk.

Following the Secret Sermon are more than a dozen parables about heaven:

The kingdom of heaven is like a man who sowed seed…like a mustard seed…like a treasure buried in a field…like a net in a lake…like a king settling accounts…like a landowner who hired workers…like a king who prepared a wedding banquet…like ten virgins…

Woven in between the parables are more references to heaven. Jesus explained that the least in the kingdom of heaven was greater than John the Baptist. He compared the lowly position of a child to that of the greatest in the kingdom of heaven.

And don't forget the secret hike, recounted later in Matthew (see 17:1–13), when Jesus showed Peter, James, and John a glimpse of heaven through His transfigured state. Given the amazing sight they were seeing, you really can't blame the disciples for cornering Jesus with questions such as, "Who is the greatest in the Kingdom?"

Jesus's supersized attention to heaven is understandable. Heaven is where He came from. And heaven was where He would soon return. He saw what was ahead for Him—and ahead of us.

We desperately need the benefit of His view!

Rewards at Family Camp

Well done, good and faithful servant! You have been faithful with a few things; I will put you in charge of many things. Come and share your master's happiness! (Matthew 25:21)

Throughout Matthew's gospel, each of Jesus's sermons builds momentum toward a trip to the cross. For Jesus, this means returning home to heaven. Just two days before the final events leading to His arrest and crucifixion, Jesus shared the parable of the talents: a master rewarded three servants for how they invested the abilities that were entrusted to them.

For me, the point of the story is the end of the story: all the investment, risk taking, fear, boldness, action, and inaction… It all leads to the Day! And on that Day we will receive our rewards.

God is taking note of our lives. And on the Day, we will give an account for what we did with our abilities. It matters to God how we live. The way we live today leads to rewards for tomorrow!

It's Okay to Want Rewards

Jesus's disciples didn't seem to have a problem with the idea of rewards. The disciples wanted to understand the payoff for their risky commitments. When they asked Jesus what their reward would be for their sacrifices on earth, He confirmed there would be rewards. He added that He is not the One who determines them—our Father does.

After James and John, along with Peter, witnessed Jesus's transfiguration on a mountain, they very likely had some follow-up questions about heaven. Not long after the Transfiguration, the mother of James and John approached Jesus with a request. She wanted her sons to sit next to Jesus, one on either side of Him, when He reigned in His kingdom (see Matthew 20:21).

That's some request! (Is it just me, or do you wonder if the boys leaked details of their secret hike to their mom?) Meanwhile the other disciples caught wind of this and became irritated with James and John.

You know why this bothered them? It wasn't a theological dispute. They shared the same views about heaven. How could you not after hanging around Jesus? Instead, they were annoyed. It's similar to a parent's showing up at school to lobby for little Johnny to get a bigger part in the Christmas play. It just feels rude and improper.

To me, though, this scene is humorous. Jesus didn't rebuke the proud mother or her sons. Instead, He pulled the disciples aside and helped them understand how things will unfold. One day, rewards will be distributed in heaven: the ways you use your time, efforts, gifts, and talents today determine where you will be seated in heaven.

God wants you to want rewards!

What Are the Rewards?

For we must all appear before the judgment seat of Christ,
that each one may receive what is due him for the things
done while in the body, whether good or bad. (2 Corinthians
5:10)

But what are the rewards? Fortunately Scripture gives us some clues. For starters, there will be praise from the Father. Just like the servants from the parable who heard, "Well done good and faithful servant," you will be recognized for your service.

Maybe it will happen when you have that private moment with God, when He presents a special white stone bearing your new name (see Revelation 2:17). He has a new name picked out for you that only He and you will know. Talk about a special secret! Just between you and your Father.

Rewards will come in the form of possessions too. I'm not sure how this works, but numerous passages talk about them. Jesus tells us to be shrewd in how we use our earthly wealth so we can obtain the "true riches," also described as "property of your own" (Luke 16:11–12).

Paul told Christians living in Philippi that their gifts to him would result in credits to their heavenly account (see Philippians 4:17). And immediately following the Secret Sermon, Jesus said, "store up for yourselves treasures in heaven" (Matthew 6:20). As God's children, we will have assets in heaven.

And don't forget about new roles and assignments. Some may be elders or even worship leaders (see Revelation 5:13–14). And others will govern cities or other territories (Luke 19:17–19). These rulers will travel through the gates of the New Jerusalem (heaven's capital city) to bring their splendor into the city (see Revelation 21:24). Wild, I know!

This new Kingdom will be massive. If today's galaxies cover billions of light years, there could be quite a bit of real estate for us to explore. We'll have eternity for this adventure and will do so in orderly fashion.

Don't Just Take It or Leave It

Many people struggle with teachings about rewards. Being rewarded seems to run counter to the selfless nature we are trained to take on.

Jesus said that whoever humbles himself like a child will be great in the kingdom of heaven. He also said we would receive rewards in heaven. Putting on humility to earn something in return (heavenly rewards) seems paradoxical. But being rewarded is God's idea, not ours. If you were having lunch with Jesus and He insisted on paying, do you really think you could fight Him over the check?

Remember the full definition of faith from Hebrews 11:6. Anyone who desires to please God must (1) believe He exists and (2) believe that He rewards you if you earnestly seek after Him. To seek God's rewards is a core expression of faith, according to God.

Walking with Strangers

> Do not neglect to show hospitality to strangers, for by this some
> people have entertained angels without knowing it. (Hebrews
> 13:2, NASB)

When I was walking the grocery store aisles and pushing a shopping cart
with Mrs. Whyte, I talked with her about how someday she would have
a completely different life in heaven. She had no trouble accepting this
reality, as if she understood it better than I did. It was a reminder to me
that often my privileged "chair" in life (food, possessions, family) can
obstruct my view and hope for heaven.

After I purchased the groceries and walked her out to the bus stop, I
imparted the strange yet fitting words about sharing her food and money
with others. *"Jesus will see it, He will be pleased, and He will reward you
one day in heaven,"* I told her.

Back in the car with Austin, I said, "Take a good look at that lady.
We may be working for her in heaven one day." I took the opportunity to
explain to my six-year-old how God will give possessions and positions in
heaven. (Children seem to accept this more easily than adults do.)

As much as we can glean from the Scriptures about heaven, there are
plenty of mysteries too. Sometimes we might even experience heaven's mysteries on earth, like an early glimpse of a reward. A measure of childlike
faith goes a long way in keeping you looking up and expecting more in your
walk with God. My gut says that you're feeling some childlike hope too.

Three Blinks

Back when I was fasting and praying for forty days, I mentioned that I
went to visit my elderly great-aunt, Katheryn. I took the fire-hose ap-

proach to sharing the gospel, but nothing ever happened that I could see. Five years later Aunt Katheryn was on her deathbed. She was in her nineties, had suffered a stroke, and was expected to pass any day.

I visited the room where she spent her days and nights in a bed, lying in the same position until a nurse came to reposition her body. I was told Katheryn was not responding to people; the caretakers were not sure what she could understand.

I walked over and grabbed her hands, leaned closely to her face, and spoke into her ear. She couldn't move her head, but her eyes opened and slowly rolled toward me. I got in her direct line of sight.

"Aunt Katheryn, do you remember our conversation many years ago?" She couldn't nod, but her eyes suggested she might be tracking. "Do you remember our talk about Jesus? Well, you can have that life we talked about. A life in heaven with Jesus…forever.

"Jesus is here with you. He can take you to His home when your time comes."

This was an awkward conversation. There were no nods of the head to show she was following the conversation, but no glazed look to suggest she wasn't. How could I lead Aunt Katheryn to Jesus in her condition?

I just kept talking.

"Aunt Katheryn, Jesus loves you, and you don't need to be afraid. If you'd like to go home to be with Jesus, you can reach out to Him right now." She was in no position to respond in normal ways. Then I had a thought.

"Aunt Katheryn, if you'd like to go live with Jesus forever, blink three times. Let me see three blinks…and Jesus will see it too." I waited a few long seconds, and there it was. The first blink.

"There's one, Aunt Katheryn. Give me two more blinks. After a brief pause came the second blink, then the third. I assured her that I had seen her three blinks and that Jesus had too. Her face seemed to relax slightly while the rest of her body remained motionless.

I don't know why I requested three blinks. I've learned to trust that such sudden thoughts often are planted by the Father. And for Aunt Katheryn, who had lain motionless for a long period of time, a few blinks seemed like a fair request. My great-aunt still had a chance to reach out to God.

Four days later Aunt Katheryn passed away. Only God knows what needed to happen for her to give her heart and soul to Him.

Soon

On the last page in my Bible, Jesus issued a final reminder: "Behold, I am coming soon! My reward is with me, and I will give to everyone according to what he has done" (Revelation 22:12). He had said it dozens of times already, then He said it again. We can't miss this truth: Jesus is coming back…soon! We should look forward to heaven in eager anticipation, not give up hope.

I don't know how soon "soon" is. In light of eternity, it has been only a flash since these words were recorded.

And just in case we need a final reminder of this most important idea, Jesus gave us another. The second to last verse in the Bible says, "Yes, I am coming soon" (Revelation 22:20).

Hope Again

When I had first let the news slip that we would be returning to family camp, Gunnar had been ecstatic. Then I snuffed out his enthusiasm, and I felt really bad.

I found the picture book that had ignited Gunnar's memories. When

I opened to the page of my son's camouflage face painting, my heart melted. He was so cute, so young, so excited, so hungry and in love with life. I was sorry that I had robbed him of the anticipation.

The trip was still two months away—an eternity for a little boy. But I wanted to see that spark back in his eyes. I didn't care if he bugged me every day. I didn't care if I had to go on explaining words such as *today, tomorrow,* or *next week.* So I did what I should have done in the beginning.

I picked up my little boy and put him on my lap. I looked into his eyes and told him, "Gunnar, let's look through your pictures together. We need to get ready because we're going back to family camp! *Soon!*"

Look for a
Buzzer-Shot Moment

There is no greater joy for a parent than to know his or her child is walking with God. John the disciple felt this way about his spiritual children (see 3 John 1:4). I can only imagine that God feels this way about us.

My faith foundation has been built over decades, and I trust it will continue to strengthen as my walk with God deepens. This will require more secret encounters and more buzzer-shot messages from God. I need them!

But my children will have to build their own foundation. They must seek out their own encounters with God. They must endure their own seasons of living-in-the-channel while pushing for breakout moments. They can't rest on my experiences or their mother's walk with an invisible God.

Ever since my oldest child was born, I have prayed for God's loving protection and favor in the lives of my children. I have pleaded for God to notice them in the ways we all want to be noticed—by shining His spotlight attention on them. And I pray that my children notice God noticing them, strengthening their walk with Him.

God knows this burden weighs on my heart. While watching Gunnar's basketball game on that Saturday morning, I did desire a fresh connection between God and me. But there was something else that was bottled up in my prayers from the bleachers, something I haven't fully explained until now.

While I longed for a sign that God sees *me,* what I specifically wanted from God was a sign that His eyes were shining on my son Gunnar. I wanted a clear indication that when the eyes of the Lord range throughout the earth, He sees my youngest son. This is the same prayer I say regarding each of my children—that just happened to be Gunnar's moment.

When the buzzer sounded and the ball fell through the net, I nearly forgot I was watching a basketball game. Instead, I was watching God, as God was watching Gunnar. God was letting me know, *Jeffrey, I know your heart's desire…and I've got him covered.*

That's when I heard the Applause.

God is watching you too. Yes, faith and belief are necessary. But as I mentioned at the outset, sometimes your faith needs proof, the kind you only get through your special connections with God. You can have your moment with God, that moment when you feel His pleasure, sense His delight, and hear His divine applause.

Your buzzer-shot moment of connection might be floating a touchdown pass, nailing a big presentation, or watching a child hit every note in a piano recital. It could be the right words that come just when they are needed in a conversation with a loved one, a friend, or even a stranger. Or the spontaneous guidance you need to find the spouse God has for you—without having to travel by camel.

Your connecting moment could be a song on the radio, a perfectly timed phone call or text, or the message on a billboard you noticed as you drove through town. It might be a moment that brings an unfamiliar feeling inside that swells your heart with joy, or one that brings an unexpected tear to your eye.

Your connection moment may be a particular verse that jumps off the page of your Bible. I don't know how your God-connecting moments will occur. Nor do I know how my future moments will be revealed. (Yes, I'm expecting more.)

However your connection happens, God wants you to hunger for these moments. He wants you to seek His face. Yes, the face of God, which can't be seen. But look for Him anyway.

God wants you to want rewards in your walk with Him. He likes it when you pursue crazy things such as blameless living. He wants you to start a new file of secret experiences that you share only with Him.

God's watching you to see if you're watching for Him.

Look up now. What do you see?

What do you hear?

Keep seeking and you'll find the very thing you're looking for: God's spotlight of attention...and His divine applause.

Energize Your Walk with God

Let's take some more steps together:

www.DivineApplause/walk

**Share free downloads and group resources
with your friends and your church.**

About the Author

JEFF ANDERSON speaks and writes about walking with God, using an approach that combines scripture and story.

Jeff began his career working as a CPA for a Big Six accounting firm, almost detoured into playing professional black-jack, then became a day-trader in the stock market. Following that, he joined Crown Financial Ministries as vice president for North America Generosity Initiatives.

Along the way, Jeff discovered a knack for speaking and teaching—helping people walk more closely to an Invisible God. His writing career began with a passion for Bible study that has grown for twenty years.

In 2010 he launched AcceptableGift.org where he speaks, writes, and consults with churches and ministries in the area of financial giving.

Jeff blogs about walking with God at JeffAndersonWalking.com, where you'll hear more about his wife, Stephanie, and their four children: Austin, Cade, Gunnar, and Autumn.

When he's not writing, speaking, or daydreaming, Jeff can be found watching Andy Griffith reruns with his kids, conducting miniature-golf clinics, taking family road trips, or maybe coaching a junior high track team.

No Guilt. No Pressure.
Just the Delight of Giving.

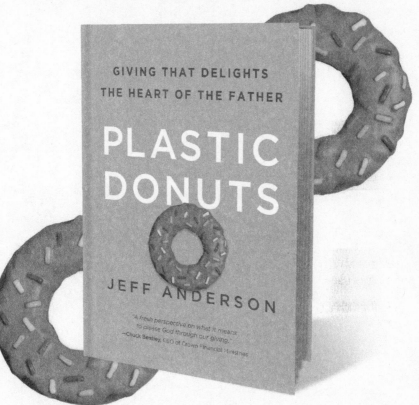

GIVING THAT DELIGHTS
THE HEART OF THE FATHER

PLASTIC DONUTS

JEFF ANDERSON

"A fresh perspective on what it means
to please God through our giving."
—Chuck Bentley, CEO of Crown Financial Ministries

When it comes to financial giving, there is more to pleasing God than a budget and a clean tithing record. Using the Plastic Donut as a metaphor, Jeff Anderson captures an approach to giving that discards pat answers while uncovering biblical truths. More importantly, Anderson shows that as you gain confidence in your understanding of giving, your connection with the Father grows stronger. Once you see your gifts from God's perspective, your giving will never be the same.

**Read an excerpt from this book and more
at WaterBrookMultnomah.com!**